ANTARCTIC OBSESSION

The Managing Owner
Sir Clements Markham.

ANTARCTIC OBSESSION

A personal narrative of the origins of the
British National Antarctic Expedition
1901–1904

by

SIR CLEMENTS MARKHAM

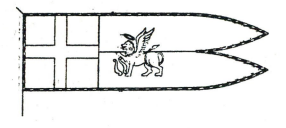

EDITED AND INTRODUCED BY
CLIVE HOLLAND

BLUNTISHAM BOOKS · ERSKINE PRESS

1986

First published in 1986 by
Bluntisham Books and the Erskine Press
Alburgh, Harleston, Norfolk IP20 0BZ

© Introduction Clive Holland 1986
Text Bluntisham Books 1986
Manuscript Scott Polar Research Institute

British Library Cataloguing in Publication Data

Markham, *Sir* Clements
   Antarctic obsession: the British National
   Antarctic Expedition 1901–1904.
   1. British National Antarctic Expedition
   (1901–1904)
   I. Title   II. Holland, Clive
   919.8'904   G850.   1902.   B7

ISBN 0 948285 09 5

Filmset in Linotron Baskerville 10 on 12pt
by Waveney Typesetters, Norwich and
Printed in Great Britain by
Antony Rowe Limited
Chippenham

THE STARTING

OF

THE

ANTARCTIC EXPEDITION

A PERSONAL NARRATIVE.

by

SIR CLEMENTS MARKHAM

K.C.B. (Arctic Medal)

1893 — 1903

The Postage Stamp
of the
Antarctic Expedition

CONTENTS

INTRODUCTION

I

The career of Sir Clements Markham is almost unique in providing a living and active connection between several of the most outstanding periods of British polar exploration spanning nearly three-quarters of a century. As he is swift to point out in this *Personal Narrative*, he was acquainted with members of Sir James Clark Ross's pioneering Antarctic expedition of 1839–43 which discovered Ross Island and Victoria Land – regions which were to become the focus of Markham's attention in later life. He had no other direct connection with this expedition, however, for he was only nine years old when it sailed. His own first experience of polar exploration was in another major period of discovery: the search for Sir John Franklin's missing North-west Passage expedition of 1845–8, during which, over some 12 years, much of the Canadian Arctic archipelago was explored for the first time. His role was a modest one, as a midshipman on the *Assistance* during Captain H. T. Austin's search expedition of 1850–1, but the experience was evidently enough to confirm his enduring interest in the polar regions. His next Arctic role, to which he also refers in the *Personal Narrative*, was in the organization of the British Arctic Expedition of 1875–6, the primary objects of which were the attainment of the North Pole and the exploration of northern Greenland and Ellesmere Island. Markham accompanied the expedition as a guest as far as south-west Greenland. Finally came his long campaign for the renewal of Antarctic exploration, which had lapsed since Ross's voyage. The culmination of that campaign was the launching of the National Antarctic Expedition of 1901–4 – the subject of this *Narrative* – and of its sequel, the British Antarctic Expedition of 1910–13 (better known as Scott's last expedition). Few men of his time could claim such prolonged involvement in polar affairs. His direct experience of the polar regions was sparse beside that of such contemporaries as Sir Leopold McClintock or Sir Vesey

Hamilton, or of Sir William Parry or Sir George Back of an earlier era, all of whom, like Markham, became distinguished advisors on polar exploration in later life; but none quite had Markham's campaigning instincts or his flair for background organization and intrigue, and none wrote so prolifically as he on polar matters. Thus, when we are confronted with Markham's previously unpublished, indeed largely private, reminiscences on the organization of the expedition closest to his heart, they merit our attention not only as a new and detailed account of the planning of this major Antarctic expedition, but also as an illuminating record of the thoughts and workings of one of the most remarkable of all promoters of polar exploration. It is with that in mind that Sir Clements Markham's *Personal Narrative* of the National Antarctic Expedition of 1901–4 has now been prepared for publication.

Clements Robert Markham was born on 20 July, 1830 at Stillingfleet in Yorkshire, second son of the Reverend David F. Markham, Vicar of Stillingfleet, and of Catherine Frances Nannette Markham, née Milner. In 1838 the family moved to Great Horkesley in Essex, where Markham's father had become Rector. When nearly nine years old Markham was sent to preparatory school at Cheam. There, according to his biographer and cousin, Albert Hastings Markham, he read the narratives of Parry's Arctic voyages which instilled in him his great interest in polar exploration. There, too, he first exercised a lifelong practice by writing a short description of each of his fellow pupils and masters; later he would continue the habit with potted biographies of all his shipmates in the navy, with his *Arctic Navy List* (London and Portsmouth, 1875), and in this present narrative with a short account of all the men of *Discovery*.

Markham left Cheam in April 1842 and in the following month he entered his secondary education at Westminster School. He remained at Westminster for only two years, for in May, 1844 Rear-Admiral Sir George Seymour, a Lord of the Admiralty and a friend of Markham's aunt, the Countess of Mansfield, invited him to join the Royal Navy. Markham accepted, and on 28 June, 1844 he travelled to Portsmouth to enrol as a Naval Cadet. His first ship was Sir George Seymour's flagship HMS *Collingwood* which, on 20 July, Markham's 14th birthday, set sail for a tour of the Pacific station, where Seymour was Commander-in-Chief. The voyage lasted four years and took in visits to Chile and Peru, the Sandwich Islands (Hawaii), Tahiti and Mexico. Halfway through the voyage, on 28 June, 1846, Markham was advanced to the rank of midshipman. The voyage appears to have left Markham with a mixture of both pleasurable and disagreeable impressions. On the one hand he enjoyed the comradeship of his messmates and made many friends; he also revelled in the experience of visiting distant places and developed a keen interest in geography. On the other hand he was less than content with some of the harsher aspects of naval discipline, not least when they rebounded against him. At times when particularly angered by some incident he would become moody, rebellious and neglectful of his duties, which in turn more than once earned him a rebuke from his commander. Those characteristics of moodiness and rebelliousness in the face of some real or imagined injustice seem to have stayed with him for the rest of his life. So, indeed, did his distaste for excessively harsh discipline: some 40 years later he initiated a campaign for the abolition of flogging in the navy. On his return home in 1848 he told his father of his dissatisfaction and expressed a wish to leave the service, but for the time being he was persuaded not to.

Markham's next appointment was on HMS *Sidon* on the Mediterranean station, but his service there was of only short duration and by the end of March 1849 he was back at Portsmouth. There then followed a full year of inactivity on board HMS *Superb*, lying at anchor at Spithead and in Cork Harbour. The experience served only to strengthen Markham's resolve to leave the navy. While at Cork, however, he had the pleasure of meeting Sherard Osborn, an old messmate from the *Collingwood*, who was then awaiting an appointment to command HMS *Pioneer* on an expedition to the Canadian Arctic in search of Sir John Franklin. Osborn succeeded in firing Markham's enthusiasm for the venture, and promised to use such influence as he had to secure an appointment for Markham also. In consequence, Markham was appointed as midshipman to HMS *Assistance*, Captain Erasmus Ommanney, in a fleet of four ships commanded by Captain Horatio Austin.

The expedition sailed on 4 May, 1850. In preparation for his forthcoming experience Markham read every Arctic book that he could lay hands on, and soon became known as an authority on Arctic history. The ships wintered in Barrow Strait in the heart of the Canadian Arctic islands, and in the spring of 1851 man-hauling sledge parties searched in all directions for traces of the Franklin expedition. Though unsuccessful in its main object, the expedition discovered several hundred miles of new coastline, and in any other circumstances might have been considered an outstanding success. For Markham, few experiences could have been better suited to his tastes. There was not only the excitement of discovery but also, just as important to him, there was the camaraderie and enthusiasm of colleagues united in a common cause, the team spirit and discipline of the sledge parties, and a winter routine which gave full rein to his creative talents. He contributed regularly to the winter newspaper, took part in the theatricals, and played a leading role in the programme of school lessons and lectures. There is no doubt that this expedition permanently shaped Markham's thoughts on how a polar expedition ought to be conducted, and consequently shaped the organization of Antarctic expeditions that were still 50 years in the future.

Despite his evident enjoyment of the Arctic expedition in all its aspects, after his return home in October 1851 Markham determined to carry out his resolve to leave the navy. There may appear to be something contradictory in his choosing to leave at a time when his enjoyment of the service was at its height, but A. H. Markham advances the view that it was just at this point that the prospect of returning to the harsher discipline of regular service must have appeared most oppressive to him. He valued the many good friends he had made in the navy, and to the end of his days he was to champion the belief that the only proper polar expedition was one conducted by highly skilled and disciplined naval officers, yet the unpleasantness of some aspects of routine naval life – A. H. Markham cites in particular the excessive punishments inflicted on the men – were clearly not to his liking. So, after passing his gunnery examinations on 24 December, 1851, he withdrew from the navy.

In 1852–3 Markham conducted an expedition to Peru to study both its geography and the history of the Incas. For several years thereafter he worked at the India Office in London. In that period he was elected a Fellow of the Royal Geographical Society on 27 November, 1854, and on 23 April, 1857 he married Minna Chichester. His work at the India Office drew to his attention the prevalence of malaria on the sub-continent, which led him to conceive a plan to carry seeds and saplings of the cinchona tree from South America to India in order to provide a local source of quinine. Consequently, at the request of the Secretary of State for India, Markham and four companions left for different parts of South America to collect the plants in December, 1859. Markham himself chose to return to Peru, and remained there for the first six months of 1860 successfully gathering cinchona in the face of much hardship and local opposition: he had virtually to smuggle his precious collection out of the country. The cinchona venture might have been the high point of any man's career. It was the first major step towards the control of malaria in India, and would alone have secured his place in history. Yet at its conclusion Markham was still only 30 years old and he still had some 50 years of achievement before him.

When he had finally completed his part in the project and returned to England in April, 1861, Markham was appointed private secretary to the Secretary of State for India. He also rose to prominence at the Royal Geographical Society, where in 1863 he was made Honorary Secretary. He retained that position for 25 years until his retirement in 1888. For several years after his return from India he was fully occupied by his work at the India Office and by the publication of various geographical works, and his next appointment overseas was not until 1867–8, when he was engaged as geographer to a British military expedition to Abyssinia. For his services in that campaign, and for his work in India, he was created a Companion of the Bath on 17 May, 1871. He became a KCB in 1896 in recognition of his geographical work.

On his reurn from Abyssinia Markham again devoted much of his spare time to geographical and historical matters, in particular his work for the Royal Geographical and Hakluyt societies. Increasingly, now, his attention was drawn by the polar regions, and especially by a plan to revive British interests in polar exploration, which had lapsed since the ending of the Franklin search in 1859, by sending out a major new Arctic expedition. The build-up towards this expedition has several interesting parallels with the organization of the National Expedition of 1901–4. Both, for example, were preceded by a prolonged campaign to arouse national and government interest, though in this case the prime mover was not so much Markham as his old friend Sherard Osborn, who first read a paper at the Royal Geographical Society in 1865 arguing for the exploration of the unknown region around the North Pole by way of Smith Sound. In both cases, too, the campaign was supported by the Royal Geographical Society which unsuccessfully approached the government for financial support. Then came the organization of a joint committee of the Royal Geographical and Royal societies, on which Markham served for both expeditions, followed by a final and successful appeal for government support. In the case of the Arctic expedition of 1875–6 the government decided upon a full-scale naval expedition financed entirely by the Treasury, so its final preparation was taken out of the hands of the two societies and entrusted to a committee of three naval officers and Arctic veterans, Osborn, F. L. McClintock and G. H. Richards. Markham nevertheless continued to busy himself with details of equipment and manning, and he was rewarded for his perseverance by an invitation from the officers to accompany the expedition as far as Greenland. The expedition, commanded by Captain George S. Nares on HMS *Alert* and *Discovery*, sailed on 29 May, 1875. Markham left it at Disko Island and returned home on the tender *Valorous*. The two expedition ships wintered at the northern end of Ellesmere Island, and in spring 1876 sledge parties explored the northern coasts of Ellesmere Island and Greenland. An attempt on the North Pole, led by A. H. Markham, failed badly, reaching only 83°20′26″N. Moreover, by the summer of 1876 the expedition was badly afflicted with scurvy, so on its reurn home later that year its undoubted successes were somewhat overshadowed by its shortcomings. In retrospect, its lack of greater success is hardly surpising. The restraining hand of the Arctic veterans on the organizing committees, Markham among them, ensured that the expedition was almost a carbon copy of those fine old expeditions of the 1850s, with little advance in either equipment or technique. There were the same great, heavy man-hauled sledges that rendered impossible any hope of reaching the Pole. There was the same old winter routine, the same sledge flags and mottoes to invoke the same rather laboured esprit de corps so beloved by Markham. And there was scurvy, the curse that had destroyed the Franklin expedition of 1848, a result of over-dependence on preserves and too much faith in lime juice. It was as if nothing had been learned in the intervening 25 years, and the longevity of some of those Arctic veterans of the '50s was to ensure that little more would be learned in the next 25 years before the despatch of the National Antarctic Expedition.

Administration and scholarly works were now increasingly Markham's main preoccupations, though he still travelled widely, and still had time to indulge in other interests. In the early 1880s he launched his ultimately successful campaign aimed at the ending of flogging in the Royal Navy. It was in the 1880s, too, that he quietly began to lay his plans for the renewal of Antarctic exploration, though it was not until he was rather unexpectedly elected President of the Royal Geographical Society, on 13 November, 1893, that those plans began to take their final shape. On becoming President he almost immediately announced his determination to launch an Antarctic expedition during his term of office, and at his first Council meeting he appointed a committee to report on matters bearing on the despatch of an expedition. The progress of his plans are the subject of his *Personal Narrative*, and some aspects of them are discussed later in this introduction, so there is no need to enlarge on them here.

The expedition was organized very much in the pattern of the large naval expeditions of the 1850s and 1870s with which Markham was so familiar, despite urgent demands from some quarters for a more modern scientific approach. It was led by Commander Robert Falcon Scott, RN, on the specially built ship *Discovery*, and it sailed on 6 August, 1901. Markham had selected as its destination the Ross Sea sector of the Antarctic discovered by James Ross in 1839–43, and it was there, at Hut Point on Ross Island, that Scott set up his winter quarters in January, 1902. From there, sledging parties explored to the south-west and to the north and one, led by Scott, travelled south over the Ross Ice Shelf to achieve a latitude of 82°17'S, a record for that time. In the summer of 1902–3 *Discovery* remained immovably fast in the ice and, instead of returning to New Zealand as planned, Scott was obliged to spend a second winter in the Antarctic. Further sledge parties explored in Victoria Land in summer 1903. *Discovery* was freed from the ice in February 1904 and joined the relief ships *Morning* and *Terra Nova* for a triumphant return home. Its main results were geographical, geological and biological discoveries in the Victoria Land region, and Markham was later to claim that 'never has any polar expedition returned with so great a harvest of results!' It was, nevertheless, conducted with a minimal scientific staff and its scientific results were modest beside those of some smaller and more efficient expeditions of the same period.

In 1905, after the winding up of the expedition, Markham resigned as President of the RGS. He was now 75 years old and entitled to a less stressful role in the world of exploration and discovery. Yet he continued to write prolifically to the last and to express his views on Antarctic affairs. He willingly collaborated with Scott in the preparations for his second Antarctic expedition, the British Antarctic Expedition of 1910–13, and he lived to learn of its tragic outcome. Markham died on 30 January, 1916 following an accident in which he set light to his bedding while reading by the light of a candle.

II

The *Personal Narrative* which forms the subject of this book is, as readers will quickly realize, more than just an account of the organization of the National Antarctic Expedition of 1901–4; it is a revelation of the inner mind of Markham himself, with all its affection and loyalty for those whom he liked, and all its venomous contempt for those he did not. His cousin Albert Hastings Markham writes endearingly of 'his personal charm and lovable disposition' and of his 'wondrous kindness and sympathy for those in trouble and distress'[1] and the evidence leaves little doubt that he possessed all those qualities. But in matters of polar exploration, when some instinct invariably told him that only he was right, he could be as obsessive, obstinate and cantankerous as any man in pursuit of his own ends. One could even agree with Roland Huntford's assessment that 'he had developed mild *folie de grandeur*. He believed he had a prescriptive right to control Antarctic exploration',[2] except that in this case it was not all Antarctic exploration he sought to control, but just one expedition. (Although he certainly did aspire to a wider control, and was brutally scornful of such men as Borchgrevink, Bruce, Shackleton and Amundsen who saw fit to organize Antarctic expeditions without his authority.)

Thus it must be stated, though the warning is hardly necessary, that this is very much a one-sided view of the origins of the expedition. That is not to say that it is inaccurate, and it is not the purpose of this introduction to redress the balance in every instance where Markham appears to express his mind unfairly. The necessary balance is provided in the appendices to this book, where Markham's adversaries are allowed to have their say.

Much of Markham's narrative is an occasionally tetchy but otherwise straightforward account of the planning and first stages of the National Antarctic Expedition. The rest is given over to a very personal view of the various committees appointed to organize the expedition, most notably the Joint Committee of the Royal Society (RS) and the Royal Geographical Society (RGS). If Markham's colourful account leaves the impression that there was much dissension and bad feeling within those committees, then the impression is most certainly correct. Even the otherwise rather conservative Dr H. R. Mill, librarian of the RGS at the time, was forced to concur with Markham's opinion that the dissensions 'nearly wrecked the expedition'.[3]

At the heart of the matter was a fundamental disagreement between the representatives of the RS and the RGS over the relative roles of the naval staff and the civilian scientific staff of the expedition. Markham, and most of the 'Arctic Admirals' of the RGS, all veterans of Arctic exploration in the 1850s and 1870s, took the traditional view that the naval interests should predominate both at sea and on land, though conceding that a small scientific staff should take charge of geological, biological and physical studies on land. The Royal Society's representatives took the opposing view that the scientific staff should have absolute responsibility for research on land under the leadership of their chosen scientific director, John Walter Gregory, a distinguished geologist. The naval staff would have been reduced to little more than ferrymen under their plan, though they accepted that the naval leader, Commander Scott, would have overall command of the expedition. The main crisis, and its outcome, were summed up by H. R. Mill in 1930. Referring to the events of February–May, 1901, he wrote:

The *Discovery* was launched at Dundee by Lady Markham and brought round to the Thames to be fitted out. Then a storm broke which nearly wrecked the expedition. The members of the Joint Committee split on the functions of the Scientific Director. Those of the Royal Society held that a man of Gregory's scientific standing and long experience as an explorer should be the unfettered leader of the land parties of the expedition, while, of course, subordinate to Scott when on board ship. The Admirals on the R.G.S. side would not hear of this, and Markham supported them. The naval leader, he said, must be in absolute command on land as well as at sea, and must never be called upon to entrust the safety of his naval ratings to any civilian. The representatives of the Royal Society rose as one man in defence of the dignity of Science. Markham became ill with the strain and worry, and the Council of the Royal Geographical Society passed resolutions in his absence which pleased him so little that on his return he secured a vote rescinding them and cancelling the Minutes. For a moment it seemed as if the Council of the Society was to split like the Joint Committee, but here the team spirit asserted itself and the President was brought to see that the conciliatory methods quietly concerted by Goldie and Darwin were the wisest. Then at the eleventh hour the crisis passed.

Gregory resigned from the expedition, the centre of gravity of which shifted from research to adventure.[1]

The 'storm' described by Mill is a reference to the Joint Committee's re-writing of the instructions to the commander of the expedition which Markham himself had drafted. Markham mentions the 'mangling' of those instructions in his narrative, but he presents only his own draft and the final version. The 'mangled' version, or more correctly the modified 'mangled' version as finally accepted by the Joint Committee, is therefore presented in Appendix 1. If it had prevailed, it would certainly have profoundly altered the nature of the expedition in a manner which Markham would never have approved. His vision of a primarily naval expedition placed the greatest emphasis on tasks in which his chosen naval staff were most skilled: geographical discovery, surveying and charting, and magnetic, meteorological and astronomical observations. He envisaged the whole expedition wintering in the Antarctic, employing the skills of naval personnel in exploration and discovery on land as well as at sea, just as in the Arctic expeditions of old. The Joint Committee's instructions, on the other hand, gave predominance to the landing and wintering of the civilian scientific staff, and particularly enjoined the naval commander not to risk wintering in the Antarctic with his ship, thus taking away from him most of the glory of Antarctic exploration and discovery.

It is certainly arguable that the amended instructions, with Gregory as leader of the land party, might have ensured a more successful expedition. Whereas Scott went to the Antarctic without previous experience of exploration or expedition leadership, Gregory had a sound record not only as a scientist but also as an explorer and leader. In 1892 he had taken part in an expedition to explore northern Kenya; when that expedition was ruined by transport difficulties and dissensions, Gregory stepped in to reorganize it as a private venture and successfully completed a pioneering study of the Great Rift Valley and the glaciers of Mount Kenya. Four years later, he took part in the first crossing of Spitsbergen with Sir Martin Conway. Gregory was also a mountaineer with experience in the Alps and a knowledge of glacier travel. There is little doubt that he could successfully have led a land party that might have achieved more scientifically, and also perhaps more in terms of exploration, than the expedition was to do without him. As Mill has said, his resignation, which followed the reinstatement of Markham's original instructions, shifted the emphasis from research to adventure. Roland Huntford, in his *Scott and Amundsen*, has gone a step farther to suggest that it damaged more than just one expedition. He claims that, by manoeuvring Gregory's resignation,

> Sir Clements Markham had changed the course of British Polar exploration. Had Gregory got his way, scientists and civilians would have taken over, and a breath of fresh air would have entered. Sir Clements upheld naval domination and ensured, at a critical time, the rule of regimented mediocrity.[5]

Certainly an opportunity had been lost to change from the pattern of unwieldy and expensive naval expeditions which had been the primary feature of British polar exploration since the 1820s, to more lightweight and more scientifically-based ventures which had been preferred for some decades by other exploring nations. But it can also be argued that this was neither the right expedition, nor the right stage of its preparation, with all the other details almost completed, to make such a major change. As Markham was later successfully to argue, it would have been a fundamental departure from the style of expedition for which funds had already been attracted from subscribers, and the RGS would hardly have been willing to invest a large portion of its own capital in an expedition which no longer had exploration and discovery as its primary objectives.

Markham was by no means the only RGS representative to oppose the amended instructions; others opposed them not only for their content but also for the manner of their presentation. At meetings of the Joint Committee between 8 February and 5 March, 1901, the RGS's representatives suddenly found themselves confronted with a series of amendments which had clearly been carefully considered by the RS's side, but of which the RGS had had no warning whatever. Moreover, it became apparent that those amendments were being pushed through as a matter of urgency not only to suit Gregory's requirements, but also to suit his convenience, as he wanted to see the amendments approved before his imminent departure for Australia. To the RGS representatives, Gregory was still a shadowy figure, and they had so far been offered 'not a particle of proof'[6] of his fitness for the post of scientific director. It now became intolerable for several of them to find that this stranger was virtually promoting himself to the leadership of the expedition through the agency of a small group of allies at the RS. Markham refused to attend any further meetings of the Joint

Committee, and three of its leading admirals resigned: Sir Vesey Hamilton, Sir Albert Markham, and Sir Anthony Hoskins. Presenting their reasons for resigning, they concluded:

> During the recent meetings of the Joint Committee it was only too palpable to us that the interests of Geographical research were subordinated to the personal interests of Dr. Gregory, and to the investigation of scientific matters which, in our estimation, are of less importance than Geographical Exploration for which the ship has been specially constructed at great expense.[7]

Markham's response was more forceful. He declined to sign the new instructions, which was required of him in his capacity as President of the RGS, and took his complaint to the RGS Council:

> It appears that Dr. Gregory went to his R.S. Friends and threatened to resign if his demand was not complied with that he should have command of a landing party. Meetings of the R.S. Members were held, without the knowledge of their R.G.S. colleagues, and the alterations were arranged in the Instructions in compliance with Dr. Gregory's demand. Then the arrangement was sprung upon us, with the intention of forcing it through at one sitting: it was in fact forced through by the majority at a second sitting. Dr. Gregory was then informed by a deputation that his demand was complied with. . . . The protegé was to have his demands complied with *first*, all other considerations to be treated of *afterwards*, or not at all. There can be only one word for such a proceeding.[8]

Markham then persuaded both societies to appoint a Select Committee of six men to re-examine the instructions and that committee, as Markham describes in his narrative, restored the original instructions almost as Markham had drafted them. That information was cabled to Gregory in Melbourne in May, 1901, and Gregory promptly cabled back his resignation.

It is strange that this extraordinary affair should have erupted at such a late stage in the planning of the expedition, for it must have been apparent much earlier that Markham and Gregory were headed on a collision course. As early as 1899 Gregory was expressing his dissatisfaction that 'the scientific staff will be quite subordinate to the naval. The naval people all hang together and regard the scientific work with indifference. The relations of the scientific and naval heads might be like those of Nansen and his captain Sverdrup.'[9] To see himself as Nansen to Scott's Sverdrup was dangerous thinking which could not possibly have fitted into Markham's scheme. He also disapproved of Scott's appointment as commander; he wrote to Edward Poulton, his closest ally on the Joint Committee, that he found Scott too inexperienced, ignorant of the basics of expedition equipment, a poor organizer, and too ready to interfere in scientific matters which Gregory considered to be solely his affair.[10] In those circumstances he might easily have resigned much earlier, but he preferred instead to seek alterations in the overall plan of the expedition to preserve his scientific work from naval interference. It was he who wanted to prevent the ship from wintering, and to keep the naval men out of the land party altogether, considering these to be necessary preconditions for performing his own duties satisfactorily. He also rejected his title 'Head of the Civilian Scientific Staff' and was prepared to go out only as 'Scientific Director'; that is, director of all science, both civilian and naval. He presented all these conditions to Poulton, who in turn led the inept and ill-fated attempt to have them incorporated in the instructions. (As it was Poulton who most vigorously represented Gregory's point of view, his own lengthy account of the affair, first published in *Nature* in 1901, is printed here in full in Appendix 2.) Poulton himself was eventually to concede that he faced special difficulties when most of the financial resources of the expedition had been raised by the RGS, and when he met with so skilful and energetic an adversary as Sir Clements Markham. It was, in the end, almost inevitable that Markham should win.

But Markham did not have everything his own way, and there was a further episode in the history of the expedition, omitted from his *Personal Narrative*, in which he finally lost control of the expedition to one of the most powerful of all adversaries: government. By winning the battle over the instructions, he had committed the *Discovery* to wintering in the Antarctic, and thereby he had also committed the two societies to purchasing and sending south a relief ship in case *Discovery* should be unable to get free of the ice at the end of winter. That required more funds, so, immediately after seeing *Discovery* on her way, Markham set about raising the sum required by public subscription. By October, 1901 he had enough to buy the ship, *Morning*, a Norwegian sealer. As with *Discovery*, the RGS was made the sole owner of the ship, and Markham, as President, was officially appointed her manager; hence his proud boast of being the expedition's 'Managing Owner'. There was still a shortage of funds for fitting out the *Morning* for her voyage south, so Markham approached the Treasury for a further grant towards the expedition. His request was refused; the government had already granted £45,000 towards the expedition and was not expecting to be asked for more. Fortunately for Markham, the money was found elsewhere, and *Morning*, under the command of William Colbeck, sailed in July, 1902. Colbeck visited Scott early in 1902, returned to Lyttelton, New Zealand, in March, and cabled home the unwelcome news that *Discovery* was still frozen in, and very probably faced the prospect of a second winter in the Antarctic; the need for a second relief expedition in 1904 was therefore 'imperative'. This left the two societies with the problem of needing to raise a further £20,000 both to keep the expedition going for another year and to send out yet another relief expedition to evacuate the whole party should *Discovery* still be frozen in. Once again they approached the Treasury for assistance. This time, reluctantly and with evident ill will, the Treasury agreed to relieve the societies of their embarrassing problem, but only on its own stringent terms which implied a complete loss of confidence in the societies' ability to manage the affair competently. Replying to their plea, the Secretary to the Treasury wrote:

> . . . after careful consideration of the difficulties in which the Royal and R.G. Societies find themselves, and in view of the necessity of providing for the safety of the officers and men of the Royal Navy who were allowed to volunteer for service on the Expedition undertaken by the two Societies, it has been decided by His Majesty's Government to offer to take over the whole responsibility for the further relief expedition which has unfortunately been rendered necessary – on condition that the existing relief ship, the *Morning*, now in New Zealand, is handed over absolutely and at once to the Board of Admiralty who will control the relief operations on behalf of the Government.[11]

To have the expedition so peremptorily removed from his control, after a decade spent planning and executing his dream, must have severely wounded Markham's pride. But he had no choice; without adequate funds there was no other way of relieving the *Discovery*. So, together with the President of the Royal Society, he wrote back agreeing to hand over the *Morning*. But in so doing he fell into a trap, for further correspondence revealed that in demanding that *Morning* be handed over 'absolutely' to the Admiralty, they were actually demanding a permanent transfer of the ownership of the vessel in order to offset some of the cost of providing relief. The Council of the RGS was unwilling to contest the issue, and on 7 July, 1903, in Markham's fortuitous absence abroad, they passed a resolution authorizing their Vice-President to transfer ownership of the *Morning* to the Admiralty. Markham was furious when he heard of this; he wrote a long and somewhat self-contradictory memorandum urging the Council to reconsider its action on the grounds that they had no authority to give the *Morning* away.

The money for the relief ship was raised by me; I bought the ship, fitted her out and despatched her, and I am the owner, every step being taken with the full approval of the Council. The *Morning* cost me 11,800*l.*; she is now worth 6000*l.* or more, with all her stores and provisions now on board, 7000*l.* This value, this valuable property, is the result of subscriptions from hundreds of sympathisers, and must be used first for the relief, second for the general needs of the expedition. The actual ownership is immaterial because it is a trust. It is not the property of the Council. Indeed, the Council did not subscribe. It is a trust to be expended for the purpose for which it was subscribed. Neither I nor the Council have any right whatever to give it away for any purpose except that for which it was entrusted to them. I cannot sign away this property, any more than can the Council.[12]

Thus did Markham pathetically cling to his last vestige of control over his Antarctic expedition; but it was to no avail. Without funds he was powerless to contest the government's terms; the relief expedition had to go out with or without his consent; and he had to step aside: the role of the Managing Owner was ended. So, too, was the role of the cumbersome, over-manned and inefficient naval polar expedition. From then on expeditions were to be smaller, cheaper, better organized, and, increasingly, platforms for science rather than adventure.

NOTE ON THE MANUSCRIPT

The original manuscript of Markham's *Personal Narrative* is in the Scott Polar Research Institute, Cambridge, England. It came to the Institute in 1983 as part of a major gift from Sir Peter Scott, son of Robert Falcon Scott. The manuscript was evidently written mainly between 1901 and 1903, but there are numerous later additions and corrections. Most noticeable are many underlinings in red, throughout the narrative, to highlight significant names, dates, and events. These underlinings have been ignored for the purposes of this transcription. Later corrections, up to about 1907, include the crossing out of favourable references to some of the persons who eventually met with Markham's disapproval. These are mostly explained in the notes at the end of the narrative. A few minor spelling and other errors have been silently corrected and some extraneous material has been left out; otherwise the manuscript has been reproduced faithfully. Most of the photographs which were pasted into the original narrative are reproduced here, as are some of his illustrations.

The manuscript was probably written mainly for Markham's own satisfaction, but its presence in the Scott family archives indicates that it may also have been written as a memento for R. F. Scott, the commander of the expedition.

Appendix 2 has been added to provide an account of events from the viewpoint of the Royal Society.

ACKNOWLEDGEMENTS

The Editor and Publishers wish to thank Sir Peter Scott for his gift of the manuscript to the Scott Polar Research Institute, and Dr David Drewry and Mr Robert Headland, Director and Archivist of the Institute, for permission to reproduce it. We also wish to thank Dr John Hemming, Director and Secretary of the Royal Geographical Society, for permission to quote from RGS copyright material in the Introduction. The journal *Nature* has kindly consented to the reproduction of an article in Appendix 2. We are also grateful to Mrs Julie Jones for her help in correcting the transcript.

THE STARTING OF THE ANTARCTIC EXPEDITION

A PERSONAL NARRATIVE

I

The objects

The Antarctic Regions were first penetrated by Sir James Ross in 1839–42, and since that time they had received no attention. The secret of the Arctic Regions was revealed by the Expedition of 1875;[1] the despatch of which was due to the united labours of myself and Admiral Sherard Osborn from 1864 to 1874. There was interesting detailed Arctic work still to be done, especially the discovery of the north coast of Greenland and of the deep sea which I believed to exist north of Franz Josef Land. From 1875 to 1885 I worked to get these problems solved, without success. Eventually Nansen, in his memorable expedition,[2] confirmed the conclusions I had formed from the results of the Expedition of 1875 combined with previous knowledge, and solved the whole Arctic mystery. He crowned and completed the labours of three centuries.

In 1885[3] I turned my attention to Antarctic exploration at which I had to work for 16 years, before success was achieved. To some extent I formed a link with the older work. In former days I knew old Mr Enderby very well, and I had many Antarctic talks with him. I also knew seven of the officers of Sir James Ross's Expedition, namely Captain Bird of the *Terror*, Lieut Phillips, Mr Tucker, Dr McCormick, Sir Joseph Hooker, Dr Lyall, and Captain Davis, the Second Master of the *Terror*, with whom I was intimate for many years. I first carefully studied the work of Sir James Ross in 1850.

While working for an Arctic Expedition, Sherard Osborn and I often discussed the Antarctic question. Captain Davis read a paper on Antarctic exploration with reference to a position for observing the transit of Venus, on Feby 22d 1869.[4] On that occasion Sherard Osborn announced that he was collecting data

[1]

for an Antarctic Expedition, to be despatched when the Arctic Expedition returned. But Osborn did not live to see its return; and I had to fight on without the aid and sympathy of my old messmate.

On March 14th 1870 Sir Vesey Hamilton read a paper on Morrell's alleged voyage, and on the use of steam in Antarctic navigation, which led to a discussion in which Captain Davis joined. At this time Davis presented a large Antarctic diagram, showing all the tracks of voyagers, to the Geographical Society. He was a most amiable trustworthy officer, a surveyor and a good artist. Davis died in 1879.

Sherard Osborn and I were agreed upon an Antarctic Expedition, and on its advantage to the country. Its main object would be the encouragement of maritime enterprise, and to afford opportunities for young naval officers to acquire valuable experiences and to perform deeds of derring doe.[5] The same object would lead to geographical exploration & discovery. Other collateral objects would be the advancement of the sciences of magnetism, oceanography, meteorology, biology, geology; but these are springes to catch woodcocks. The real objects are geographical discovery, and the opportunities for young naval officers to win distinction in time of peace.

The expedition must, therefore, be a naval expedition or, if an unenlightened Government is obdurate on this point, an expedition with as strong a naval element as possible.

II

First abortive campaign 1885–1889

At the instance of my old captain, Sir Erasmus Ommanney, the British Association, at the Aberdeen Meeting, nominated an Antarctic Committee of which I was a Member, in September 1885. It was re-nominated at Birmingham in 1886. Communications were opened with Baron Mueller and Captain Pascoe R.N. at Melbourne, who tried to influence the Government of Victoria. The result was that Sir Graham Berry, the Agent General, announced that his Government would grant £5000 if H.M.'s Government would contribute a like sum. The communication was made to the Colonial Office which received a Report from the Royal Society, and also an unfavourable reply from the Board of Trade to an enquiry respecting the trade of the Antarctic Regions. In the Autumn of 1887 I was myself collecting data relating to Antarctic work, and on November 30th 1887 I had an interview with Sir Graham Berry on the subject.

The result of the proposal of the Government of Victoria was that H.M.'s Treasury refused to grant the £5000 in a fatuous letter; and the project was dropped. Of course the sum proposed was ludicrously inadequate.

When Baron Oscar Dickson, the enlightened Swedish promoter of voyages of discovery, heard of the refusal of H.M. Treasury, he came forward and offered the £5000 if the Government of Victoria would keep to their bargain and grant the other £5000. But that Government refused; which showed their insincerity.

The command was offered to Sir Allen Young in case the proposed expedition got beyond the talking stage; but it never did.

In the meanwhile I had been considering the most important question of a commander for the future expedition. He must be a naval officer, he must be in the regular line and not in the surveying branch, and he must be young. These are essentials. Such a Commander should be a good sailor with some experience of ships under a sail, a navigator with a knowledge of surveying, and he should be of a scientific turn of mind. He must have imagination and be capable of enthusiasm. His temperament must be cool, he must be calm yet quick and decisive in action, a man of resource, tactful, and sympathetic.

The training of officers in the surveying branch is quite different from what is needed for a geographical explorer; nor is the kind of discipline and order of a surveying ship the sort of system which experience has shown to be essential for the well being of an exploring expedition. The surveying branch is not a road to promotion or distinction in the navy. Consequently those who are conscious of ability, or who are ambitious, the class of men from which a polar commander should be taken, will not join it. Such men must be selected from the regular line, generally from gunnery or torpedo lieutenants, for thither naval ability and high attainments gravitate. For to excell in these lines is the surest and quickest way to promotion. Here are the officers of ability and resource, lovers of order and discipline, accustomed to the succesful management of men, enthusiastic, ambitious, and anxious for opportunity to win a name.

In 1887 I was on board the *Active*, the guest of my cousin,[6] the Commodore of the Training Squadron, during the West Indian cruise consisting of four ships; the *Active*, *Rover*, *Volage* and *Calypso*. There were about a dozen midshipmen on board each ship. I knew well that it would take a dozen years at least before an Antarctic Expedition could be actually on foot. The midshipmen of the Training Squadron were, therefore, the future Gunnery and Torpedo Lieutenants from among whom an efficient Commander of the Expedition must be selected. I cultivated their acquaintance from this among other points of view. Allowing for changes wrought by a dozen years, I believed Tommy Smyth to be the best man in the *Active* though wanting ballast, Hyde Parker in the *Volage*, and Robert F. Scott in the *Rover*.

Two Lieutenants got up a service cutter race at St Kitts. The boats were to be at anchor with awnings spread. They were to get under way and make sail, beat up for mile, round a buoy, down mast and sail, pull down to the original place, anchor and spread awnings again. The race tried several qualities. It was on March 1st 1887. For a long time it was a close thing between Hyde Parker and Scott; but, (as Leveson declared he would, from the first) Scott won the race. On the 5th of March the winner dined with us at Barbadoes. Noel, his captain, who rarely praised any one, spoke highly of Scott. He trusted him to keep officer's watch in the day time, with the ship under sail. My final conclusion was that Scott was the destined man to command the Antarctic Expedition.[7] He was then 18.

On June 14th 1892 I was in a river steamer, going down to Greenhithe to see the boat race between the *Worcester* and *Conway* cadets. I saw on board a young *Conway* cadet who bore a remarkable resemblance to Wyatt Rawson, my *beau idéal* of a good polar officer. The boy was his nephew, son of his sister Mrs Royds. He was most anxious to get into the navy, but there were difficulties which I did my best to enable him to overcome. He became a Naval Cadet on June 30th 1892; and I looked upon Charlie Royds as another likely Antarctic officer.

When Harmsworth's expedition[8] went to Franz Josef Land, the P. and O. Company was requested to lend a good officer as navigator. Mr Albert B. Armitage, formerly a Cadet on board the *Worcester*, was selected. He dined with me on June 14th 1894; and my first impressions have been fully confirmed. Armitage is the best Antarctic navigator.

The fatal mistake, in selecting Commanders for former polar expeditions, has been to seek for experience instead of youth. Both cannot be united, and youth is absolutely essential. Elderly

[4]

men are not accessible to new ideas, and have not the energy and capacity necessary to meet emergencies. How can novel forms of effort be expected from stiff old organisms hampered by experience! Where a youthful intellect has only to grasp the new idea, the old intellect has first to comprehend the new thought, and secondly to conquer the tendency in his mind to formulate the idea in question in his old accustomed way. His powers, far from being stronger than those of young men, are considerably weaker. The inexperience and haste in decision of young leaders are disadvantages which sometimes accompany their youthful energy, but they alone have the qualities which ensure success. Old men should supply information and the results of experience, and should stay at home, making way for the younger and therefore more efficient leaders. New ideas, novel situations meet with cordial welcome when young men are at the helm. Scott was 18 in 1887, Royds 16 in 1892, Armitage 27 in 1894. These were the destined men who would be the right age when the Antarctic Expedition is ready for them.

III

The effort for a Naval Expedition 1893–1897

In May 1893 I was elected President of the Royal Geographical Society, and I resolved that the Antarctic Expedition should be despatched during my presidency. I began work at once. On October 10th 1893 I delivered an Antarctic lecture at Liverpool. On the 16th I induced Dr John Murray (*Challenger*) to open my first session with an Antarctic paper on November 23rd 1893. Murray's views were the same as mine, that there should be a Government expedition under naval discipline, consisting of two ships. The paper was a great success, the Duke of Argyll, Sir J. Hooker, Sir W. Flower, and several distinguished naval officers speaking in favour of an Expedition.[9]

The Council of the Royal Geographical Society next appointed a special Antarctic Committee to report on the subject. The Antarctic Committee consisted of eight persons:

	R.G.S. President	Sir Vesey Hamilton
	Sir Joseph Hooker	Sir E. Ommanney
never came {	Mr Leigh Smith	Sir G. Nares
	Dr John Murray	Captn Wharton RN

I drew up the Report which enumerated the objects to be

attained, discussed the questions of ice navigation; and recommended the equipment of two vessels, under naval discipline, to be away three years; and that very wide discretion should be given to the commander; and concluded by saying that 'apart from the valuable scientific results of an Antarctic expedition, great importance must be attached to the excellent effect that all such undertakings, in which our country has been prominent, have invariably had on the navy, by maintaining the spirit of enterprise.'

On February 12th 1894 this Antarctic Report was adopted by the R.G.S. Council.

At this time I made a most serious mistake by inviting the Royal Society to join the Royal Geographical Society in their Antarctic project. On that occasion (Dec 12th 1893) the reply was evasive, namely that the R.S. Council would consider the matter. That eminent body then proceeded to steal a march upon us. Their Secretary, Professor Rücker, drew up a Report on the importance of a magnetic survey in the southern regions. The Royal Society then asked the First Lord of the Admiralty to receive a deputation of their body, keeping me in ignorance of their proceedings. It was a scurvy trick, and deserved failure. They were received, but Sir William Harcourt, the Chancellor of the Exchequer, who was in the First Lord's chair; refused to listen, snubbed them well, and sent them about their business. Their object was to get the matter entirely into their own hands.

These proceedings were kept a secret from me until November 2d 1894, when Sir John Evans, the R.S. Treasurer, informed me of the Deputation and its failure, and said that I had better give up the project. I replied that I should do nothing of the kind, and proceeded to write to other leading scientific Societies, obtaining their adhesion. On December 7th 1894 I moved a resolution in favour of an Antarctic Expedition, at a meeting of the Council of the British Association with Lord Salisbury in the chair. Sir John Evans opposed on the ground of expense, suggesting that the United States might be asked to join in an international expedition. Francis Galton also opposed on similar grounds. But Lord Salisbury put my resolution to the meeting and it was carried unanimously.

On March 4th 1895 I read a paper on Antarctic discovery at the Imperial Institute with Sir Vesey Hamilton in the chair. On April 10th 1895 I read a paper on an Antarctic Expedition from a naval point of view, at the United Service Institution, with Admiral Colomb in the chair. In the discussion it received unanimous support from leading naval officers. On July 29th 1895 I passed a Resolution at the International Geographical Congress, in favour of Antarctic exploration.

The ground having been well prepared, I wrote to Mr Goschen asking him to receive a Deputation which desired to represent to him the strong reasons for despatching a naval expedition to explore the Antarctic Regions. In a long civil reply, dated November 11th 1895, the First Lord of the Admiralty declined to receive a Deputation on the ground that he had quite made up his mind that a Government expedition was out of the question. Nearly a year was then wasted, mainly owing to obstruction from Captain Wharton, the Hydrographer. But on November 10th 1896 I had an interview with Mr Goschen. He dwelt upon the impossibility, in the existing state of public affairs, of lending any officers or men, but expressed great interest in the undertaking. I, therefore, urged him to have an official letter sent to me, stating the utmost that the Admiralty could do. To this he consented.

At about this time Dr Nansen came to England, and I thought it a good opportunity of propitiating Mr Goschen. So I invited him to dinner to meet Nansen, and also the outspoken John Murray, on February 7th 1897. It may have done some good. The promised official letter came from the Secretary to the Admiralty on April 6th 1897. Their Lordships would take great interest in the work of the expedition, would give all information existing at the Admiralty, and would lend the instruments. To have got a promise of the instruments was a small point gained.

In order that no stone might be left unturned, I wrote a letter to the Prime Minister on October 25th 1897, stating the strong reasons for the despatch of a Government Expedition. Lord Salisbury replied that he would consult his colleagues. In June 1898 the final reply came refusing to send an Expedition, refusing all help, and needlessly adding that neither would the Australian Governments give any help.

IV

An Antarctic Expedition by the Two Societies
Raising of the Funds

The reply of Mr Goschen, in November 1895, proved to me that the hope of a Government Expedition must be given up. The despatch of a private expedition involved a most serious responsibility. After many consultations and much thought I decided that it was my duty to face that responsibility. But the R.G.S. Council was not at first prepared to follow me. The question was discussed on November 29th, and again at the Council meeting on December 9th, when much tedious obstruction was caused by Captain Wharton, the Hydrographer. On January 31st 1896 the Expedition Committee of the R.G.S. resolved that the time was not propitious for an attempt to get up an Antarctic Expedition. I had to bide my time. At length the R.G.S. Council came to a momentous decision. On April 12th 1897 it was resolved that an expedition should be despatched, and I was authorized to raise the necessary funds.

I began to make appeals both by circulars and private letters. I also took the opportunity of the Australian Premiers being in England for the Jubilee, to invite them and the Agents General to a conference and luncheon at 1 Savile Row. Several accepted, but they were very rude and never came. The day was July 5th 1897. After waiting a long time I opened a discussion, in which the Duke of Argyll, Sir Joseph Hooker, Professor Rücker, the Honble C. C. Bowen of New Zealand, and two Agents General took part. Lord Lothian proposed a vote of thanks to me, and the luncheon followed. The conference seemed to be a failure, but the Government of Queensland subsequently subscribed a £1000 for the fund; thus distinguishing this colony above the others, as regards patriotic generosity. In October 1897 I published an Antarctic article in the *Forum*. In the end of 1897 I made another serious mistake by inviting the Royal Society to join us, in spite of their cryptic conduct in 1895. This time they at once agreed to coalesce. It was a fatal error, but I did so under the impression that the great name of the Royal Society would bring in funds. This was a complete mistake. The coalition has been a source of worry, delays, friction and danger; and no good whatever.

The R.S. officials celebrated this unlucky coalition by a special meeting on February 24th 1898, when John Murray read a paper, and some one was told off to speak for each science. Dr Nansen was present, and Dr Neumayer from Hamburg. A dinner was given afterwards to Dr Neumayer at the Athenaeum. A small Joint Committee was then formed, to arrange about applying to the Government for a grant of money.

On June 20th 1898 the Council of the Royal Geographical

Society resolved to head a subscription list with £5000. Mr Harmsworth promised me another £5000, and by the end of the year I had raised nearly £14000. Some influential people said I should get no more, and advised me to return it. I replied that I should do nothing of the kind, and issued another circular on November 21st 1898.

I kept on writing letters to rich people; and on March 15th 1899 I received a letter from Mr L. W. Longstaff of Ridgelands, Wimbledon, asking me if a sum of £25000 would enable the expedition to start. I went to Wimbledon on the 21st and explained to Mr Longstaff that an expedition on a small scale could and would start on the £40,000 thus raised. But we agreed that his patriotic and munificent generosity would, in all probability, lead to further subscriptions from other quarters. On the 22d Mr Longstaff informed me that the £25,000 was paid. On the 27th I announced this splendid donation from one of our Fellows, at a meeting of the Geographical Society at which Lord Lister was present, who also made public recognition of Mr Longstaff's munificence.

This noble conduct altered the whole posture of affairs. The Prince of Wales had properly declined to connect himself with the expedition until the public feeling was manifest. But on April 11th His Royal Highness complied with my request to become Patron of the Expedition, and on the 13th the Duke of York became Vice Patron. On the 22d I sent out a third Circular earnestly appealing for funds.

The action of Mr Longstaff soon led to important results. Mr Balfour, the First Lord of the Treasury, was induced to consider the question and, being favorable to scientific researches, he thought that a grant might be made. Sir Francis Mowatt, the Secretary of the Treasury, was also in our favour. The Chancellor of the Exchequer yielded. It was made known that if a request was made for a deputation to be received by Mr Balfour, it would be granted.

I accordingly drafted a letter to the First Lord of the Treasury, and a statement of the expected scientific results. The letter was signed by the Presidents of the two Societies, the Presidents of other Societies, the Chancellors of the Universities, the Secretaries of Societies, Professors, and several distinguished Arctic officers – 42 signatures.

Mr Balfour received us at the Foreign Office. I introduced the Deputation in a speech, and was followed by Sir Joseph Hooker, Lord Kelvin, Professor Ray Lankester, and Professor Rücker. In his reply Mr Balfour said that expeditions towards the poles of the earth were eminently desirable both on practical and on purely scientific grounds; and that the Chancellor of the Exchequer would find it in his power to give substantial aid to the great project of Antarctic exploration. This was on June 22d 1899. On July 3d a letter from the Treasury announced that the grant would amount to £45000 provided that not less than an equal amount was forthcoming from other sources. So that there was a condition attached. We had only raised £42,000. The Government Grant would not be obtained unless we could get £3000 more. I appealed to the R.G.S. Council, and that enlightened body agreed to subscribe another £3000, making £8000 in all. The R.G.S. Council thus secured the Government Grant.

I and the Secretary continued to make appeals to the public by lectures, private letters, and circulars, and when the expedition sailed in August 1901, the subscribed funds amounted to £93,000.

V

Plan of Operations · Complement · Instructions

As soon as the Geographical Society's Council had decided, on May 10th 1897, that funds should be raised for an expedition, I began to put my notes into form and was so occupied in Norway, throughout the summer of 1897. For there was much to consider. The expedition would consist of only one ship, and the scheme would have to be less ambitious and to involve less risk than if a Government Expedition with two ships and unlimited resources had been undertaken.

A very detailed examination of all previous voyages and of all that is known of the Antarctic Regions was necessary before a plan of operations could be prepared. I divided the Antarctic Regions into 4 Quadrants – with names –

1   The Victoria Quadrant – 90°E to 180°
2   The Ross Quadrant – 180° to 90°W
3   The Weddell Quadrant – 90°W to 0°
4   The Enderby Quadrant – 0 to 90°E

After discussing all possible routes in the four Quadrants, I came to the conclusions that our plan should be to undertake the Victoria and Ross Quadrants. I read a paper on the subject at

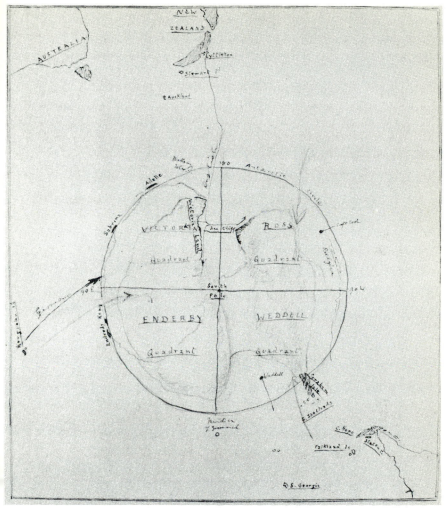

1. The Antarctic Quadrants.

the International Geographical Congress at Berlin on September 29th 1899, and on October 1st, in a conference with Erik von Drygalski, the Commander of the German Expedition, we agreed that the Germans should undertake the exploration of the Enderby Quadrant, and the English of the Victoria and Ross Quadrants. In October I wrote a more detailed paper on the routes which was published in the number of the *Geographical Journal* for July 1901, following my Anniversary Address. It contains the plan of operations which was finally adopted.

I decided that the Expedition must consist of a Commander, Navigator, three Executive Officers, and Engineer and two Surgeons making eight officers of the ship, and a ship's company of about 26 men. There must also be three scientific civilians, a geologist, a biologist, and physicist, one perhaps being placed over the others as director.

The Instructions which I drafted in 1897 were based on the plan of operations, and my conclusions respecting the complement. Its whole spirit was trust in the Commander: to state the objects it is desired to secure, and to leave their obtainment to the Commander's discretion and judgment.

The instructions commence with statements of the objects of the Expedition; and of the scientific work assigned to the executive officers and civilians. The position of the Director of the scientific civilians is laid down in the very same words as were used in the appointment of Sir Wyville Thompson to the *Challenger*. Special stress is then laid on the two principal objects, geographical discovery and the magnetic survey. The Commander is then instructed to force his ship through the pack and occupy the first navigable season in endeavouring to explore the unknown region to the eastward of the point reached by Sir James Ross in 1842, and to ascertain the nature of the great ice cap. It is left for the decision of the Commander on the spot whether suitable winter quarters can be found for the ship or whether he will put a landing party on shore; but pointing out the great importance of wintering, if all the desired results are to be secured. An alternative route is then suggested between the meridians of 110° and 160°E. The other paragraphs relate to business details, and some verbal alterations have been made in them. But in the main, and as regards all essential points, the Instructions I wrote in 1897 are the same as those under which the Expedition sailed in 1901.

I was also impressed with the necessity for sending out a relief ship after the first winter. In 1875 I wrote a pamphlet on this subject. In it I pointed out that the Franklin disaster would never have happened if a relief ship had gone out after the first winter; and that ships were sent out to Ross's expedition after the first winter, and to Belcher's expedition after the first and second winters. In 1876, after the first winter of the Nares Expedition, I urged that a relief ship should be sent out to communicate. In spite of opposition from Adml Richards the Hydrographer, my argument so impressed Mr Ward Hunt the first Lord, and Sir A. Milne, that the Admiralty undertook the duty through the instrumentality of Sir Allen Young, whose expenses in the *Pandora* were to be paid.

The arguments I used were even more applicable to the Antarctic Regions, where communication is more difficult and uncertain, and the dangers less known. It is, therefore, urgent that a relief ship should be sent out in 1902 after the first winter, and I prepared a report on this subject also, in 1897; but the time to appeal for funds will be after the expedition has started.

Thus all the most important points connected with the expedition had been fully considered and settled before the unlucky coalition with the Royal Society, and nothing has since been altered.

VI

The Appointments

Charlie Royds volunteered for the Antarctic Expedition on April 3d 1899. He was then in the destroyer flotilla at the Nore. On the 17th he was one of the three who first examined the plans for the Antarctic ship. Soon afterwards he joined the *Crescent*, flag ship of Sir Fredk Bedford on the North American Station, where he was ready for a summons at a moment's notice. I decided that he should be one of the Antarctic heroes.

The selection of the Commander of the Expedition involved the most important decision. I had never forgotten the cutter race at St Kitts, but had followed Scott's career, and on February 24th 1897 I had the pleasure of meeting him at dinner on board the *Empress of India* at Vigo. On June 5th 1899 there was a remarkable coincidence. Scott was then Torpedo Lieutenant of the *Majestic*. I was just sitting down to write to my old friend Captain Egerton of the *Majestic* about him, when he was announced. He came to volunteer to command the Expedition. I believed him to be the best man for so great a trust, either in the navy or out of it. Captain Egerton's reply and Scott's testimonials and certificates most fully confirmed a foregone conclusion.

The Government grant might well be expected to alter the views of the Admiralty on the question of lending officers and men. Admiral Sir Anthony Hoskins, to whose memory the Expedition owes so much, exerted his great influence with the two senior Naval Lords, Lord Walter Kerr and Admiral

[13]

Douglas, and they promised two officers. I then wrote to Mr Goschen on March 31st 1900, representing that the recognition of the Expedition by the Government had quite altered the aspect of affairs since I last saw him, and earnestly requesting him to take a step on which the success of the Expedition depended, by allowing officers to serve. On April 6th Mr Goschen replied that he had screwed himself up to lending two excellent officers. On the same day the Secretary of the Admiralty announced that Lieut Scott would have leave to command the expedition, with Lieut Royds as his chief executive officer. I had previously submitted the names to Lord Walter Kerr.

On June 9th 1900 Lieut Scott and on June 18th Lieut Royds were appointed to the Expedition in letters signed by the two Presidents; and on June 30th Scott was promoted to the rank of Commander. Their services were to be available from September.

Already there were indications that attempts might be made by the civilian element to encroach on the rightful position of the Commander and I was glad to find that Scott was quite resolved, from the first, to allow nothing of the kind. In this he would have my most determined support.

In a letter dated June 24th 1900 Scott laid down the conditions on which he consented to take the command.

'1. I must have complete command of the ship and landing parties. There cannot be two heads.

2. I must be consulted on all matters affecting the equipment of the landing parties.

3. The executive officers must not number less than four, exclusive of myself.

4. I must be consulted in all future appointments both civilian and others, especially the Doctors.

5. It must be understood that the Doctors are first medical men, and secondly members of the scientific staff, not *vice versâ*.

I am ready to insist upon these conditions to the point of resignation if, in my opinion, their refusal imperils the success of the undertaking.'

When Scott wrote this he was still serving on board the *Majestic*, and it gave me the greatest confidence in his firmness and clear insight. There was much intricate pilotage before the Expedition would be safe.

Armitage returned from his three Arctic winters on Franz Josef Land in 1898, and on June 5th 1899, the very day that

Scott volunteered, I had the pleasure of presenting Armitage with the Murchison Award for his scientific observations, and for his loyal and wise conduct under very difficult circumstances. I had a long conversation with him on Sunday the 28th of May 1900, and on the 29th he volunteered to join the expedition as Navigator. I thought it necessary that Scott and Armitage should know each other before there was anything definitely settled, so the latter made another voyage to China. On his return the two met, were delighted with each other, and came to a complete understanding. So in the autumn of 1900 Armitage became Second in command and Navigator, a most successful appointment, and thoroughly satisfactory in every way to the Commander. I got him promoted in the Royal Naval Reserve from Sub-Lieut to Lieutenant.

The three remaining officers were selected by Scott. Michael Barne as Second Lieutenant, Reginald Skelton as Engineer, and Ernest Shackleton as third Lieutenant. Barne and Skelton were Scott's shipmates in the *Majestic*. The former, Lieutenant of a year's standing, is a charming young fellow, so zealous that he would have thrown up his commission rather than not go, and a relation of mine[10] which is also in his favour. He volunteered on June 5th 1900.

Skelton is a stirling, able, and zealous officer, thoroughly acquainted with the scientific and practical branches of his profession, and a man of inventive genius. He will prove an invaluable member of the expedition. He is an officer who can be looked to for efficient help outside his own work as Engineer. He has the Commander's confidence, a well bred gentleman, and a good Messmate.

Scott was fortunate in finding such an excellent and zealous officer as Ernest Shackleton for third Lieutenant.[11] Son of a Doctor at Norwood, but from Ireland, his great-grandfather was the quaker Shackleton who was the instructor of Edmund Burke. But the family was originally from Yorkshire. Shackleton went to sea at the age of 16, and became a thorough seaman off the Horn and in the Pacific in sailing vessels. Latterly he had served in the Castle Line of steamers. He is a steady, high principled young man full of zeal, strong and hard working, and exceedingly good tempered. He is remarkably well informed considering the rough life he has led, and takes an interest in many subjects. I got him into the Reserve as a Sub Lieut.

The medical officers were a great difficulty. On the strong recommendation of Mr Harmsworth, who furnished me with the details of his medical career, I selected Dr Reginald Koettlitz as Surgeon. He had served during three Arctic winters in Franz Josef Land, in the Harmsworth Expedition with Armitage, and therefore has considerable Arctic medical experience. He is anxious to do his best, zealous, and painstaking and will, I believe, be a success. His mind perhaps works rather slowly, and he has no sense of humour; but on the other hand he is thorough and persevering.

Sir Charles Wilson wrote to me to recommend his nephew Dr Edward Wilson of Cheltenham for the post of Assistant Surgeon. He sent specimens of his drawings and paintings, not only of scenery, Alpine and Norwegian, but of birds and fishes, all showing a masterly hand, and delicate touch. As an Artist he will be invaluable, he is reported to be an efficient medical man, and he will be a very amiable messmate. He does not appear strong, and must be saved as much as possible from hard work and exposure. I approved his appointment in December 1900. Dr Wilson married three weeks before the Expedition started, and received a wedding present for his messmates in which I was allowed to join.

About the Director and Members of the Civilian Staff there was much friction and trouble caused by the jobbing of unpractical R.S. Professors and Hydrographers. But this will form a separate chapter, and must not be allowed to mar the orderly history of the starting of a great national Expedition. Finally the civilian staff was arranged as follows:

1. Mr Hodgson Biologist, at 36
2. Mr Ferrar Geologist, at 22
3. Mr Bernacchi Physicist, at 24

Mr Hodgson is from Birmingham, a cousin of old Sir Arthur Hodgson. He resigned the post of Curator of the Plymouth Museum to take up the appointment of Biologist in the Expedition on June 15th 1900. He is thoroughly versed in all the mysteries of dredging and fishing, and is an expert as regards the invertebrate fauna. Quiet and most attentive to his duties, Hodgson is, in his way, zealous for the success of the expedition. He is young to have a polished bald head sometimes needing a skull cap, but otherwise apparently strong and healthy. He is gifted with some quaint humour, generous, and a nice fellow.

Mr Ferrar is a geologist student from Cambridge, well versed in palaeontology, and with a good knowledge of observations connected with physical science. He is a good oarsman, and athlete and has the great advantage of youth, being only 22 – a very agreeable nice young fellow. Mr Bernacchi was born in Tasmania, and was two years at the Melbourne Observatory. He is a magnetician and physicist, a man of science of considerable ability, and he acquired Antarctic experience in the Newnes Expedition. He goes out by an Orient Steamer to join the ship at Lyttleton, bringing with him the pendulum apparatus and one of the magnetic instruments made at Potsdam. He was always a grown up – never a boy.

It is arranged that Mr George Murray F.R.S. the Head of the Botanical Department at the British Museum, is to go out as far as the Cape, as Director of the Civilian Staff, to superintend the dredging and get the work of the laboratories into efficient order. He is also to edit the scientific work on the return of the Expedition. Dr Mill went out as far as Madeira, to coach Ferrar in his physical observations.

It was Sir Anthony Hoskins to whom the Expedition was indebted for overcoming much disinclination and, by his influence, obtaining permission for petty officers and men to serve in the Antarctic Expedition. This was most important as it would be quite impossible to get anything approaching the same class of men from the merchant service. The Admiralty allowed three first class petty officers, six petty officers, nine able seamen, five stokers, two Marines, and a steward to join from the navy making, with four officers, altogether 30 naval men: with time to count for pensions, full pay and allowances, and all borne on the books of the *President*.

Mr Dellbridge, the Assistant Engineer, and two excellent petty officers, Evans and Allan, came with Scott from the *Majestic*. Mr Feather, the Boatswain, a Norfolk man, came from the *Boscawen*. The Carpenter, Mr Dailey, came from the *Ganges*. There is also a shipwright and an armourer, but they are not naval.

(The Ship's Steward, Mr Else, is not a naval man. He was in the *Windward* and was strongly recommended by Mr Harmsworth. He did not go out, remaining behind.)

Mr Ford, the Ward Room Steward, is a naval man from the *Vernon*, son of a Gunner: a very efficient person, and a good accountant. (Roper, the Cook, has won a silver medal for his cookery); and Clarke, the Cook's Mate, who will also be Laboratory Assistant, was Cook at the observatory on the summit of Ben Nevis, at the time when Charlie Royds went up there.

The Ship's Company is picked. The Commanders of the ships in the Channel Fleet called for volunteers, and selected the men best fitted for the work. The examiners said they had never seen a finer body of men. Besides – there are six merchant seamen.

47 SOULS

ANTARCTIC EXPEDITION

Naval (32)

Robert Falcon Scott
  (Commander)
Charles Rawson Royds
  (Lieutenant)
Michael Barne (Lieutenant)
Reginald Skelton (Engineer)
J. H. Dellbridge
  (Asst. Engineer)
T. Alfred Feather (Boatswain)
Frederick Dailey (Carpenter)
Edgar Evans (Petty Officer)
David Silver Allan
  (Petty Officer)
William Smythe (Petty Officer)
Jacob Cross (Petty Officer)
William Macfarlane
  (Petty Officer)
Thomas Kennar
  (Petty Officer)
James W. Dell (Able Seaman)
Jesse Handsley (Able Seaman)
William L. Heald
  (Able Seaman)

Thomas Crean (Able Seaman)
William Peters (Able Seaman)
George J. Vince (Able Seaman)
Arthur Pilbeam (Able Seaman)
Ernest E. M. Joyce
  (Able Seaman)
Frank Wild (Able Seaman)
T. S. Williamson
  (Able Seaman)
George B. Croucher
  (Able Seaman)
Gilbert Scott (Royal Marine)
Arthur H. Blissett
  (Royal Marine)
Arthur Quartly (Stoker)
William Lashly (Stoker)
Frank Plumley (Stoker)
Thomas Whitfield (Stoker)
William Page (Stoker)
C. Reginald Ford (Steward)

Royal Naval Reserve (2)

Albert B. Armitage
  (Lieutenant)

Ernest Shackleton
  (Sub Lieutenant)

Not Naval (13)

Dr Reginald Koettlitz
  (Surgeon)

William Hubert (Donkey Man)
James Duncan (Shipwright)

[18]

Dr Edward Wilson (Surgeon)   Robert Sinclair A.B.
Lewis C. Bernacchi (Physicist)   John Walker A.B.
T. V. Hodgson (Biologist)   Charles Clark (Cook)
H. T. Ferrar (Geologist)   Horace Buckridge
                                       (Laboratory Asst.)
                                    C. Hare
                                    H. R. Brett
                                    F. C. Weller (Charge of dogs)

VII

The Executive Work

FIRST PERIOD

1 April 1899 to 26 Nov. 1900

20 months

For twenty months, from 2 April 1899 to 26 November 1900, I was in charge of the executive work of the Expedition; but worried and hampered by the Royal Society's Committees, which will be described presently.

I had previously considered the question of a ship, seen all that Norway possessed, and obtained details of the Scottish whalers which sail from Dundee. My conclusion was that it would be necessary to build a ship specially for the Antarctic work.

On April 2d 1899 I wrote to Sir William White asking him to recommend me an able naval architect who would design a wooden ship for ice navigation. He advised me to employ Mr W. E. Smith, one of the Chief Constructors at the Admiralty, and the only one, except Sir William himself, who was brought up to wooden ship building. I at once put myself in communication with Mr Smith who consented to be my architect, and to prepare the plans. I then called together a Ship Committee with my old messmate Sir Leopold McClintock as Chairman, my Cousin Admiral Markham as Secretary, and Admiral Sir Anthony Hoskins, with others who did not take an active part. On April 10th my Committee met, and determined that the lines of the old *Discovery* should be followed for the new ship.

Mr Smith then proceeded with the designs. On April 17th he completed the plans, which were carefully examined by Sir Leopold McClintock, Charlie Royds, and myself, and

[19]

approved.[12] On June 20th we met again and, at the urgent request of Captain Creak, we arranged that there should be a magnetic observatory on deck, with no steel or iron within 30 feet of it, in any direction.[13] Some further details were discussed and arranged at a meeting on September 25th; and I then prepared to issue invitations to tender.

Correspondence rapidly began to accumulate, and help became necessary. On June 28th 1899 I appointed Mr Cyril Longhurst to be Secretary to the Antarctic Expedition at £1000 a year with a room at 1 Savile Row as his office, and where people could have interviews with him. His work continued to increase, there was extensive correspondence, much of it of a very confidential nature, accounts to be kept, business of various kinds to be transacted, and interviews to be given to people of all kinds. No one could have satisfactorily filled this post who was not gifted with a clear head, a good memory, great powers of application, a high sense of duty, an even temper, and some diplomatic skill. Cyril Longhurst has shown that he possesses all these qualities. His services to the expedition have been most valuable, indeed indispensable. Much of his time was wasted by having to attend all the R.S. Joint Committees and Sub-Committees, and to record their futile minutes.

After my return from the Congress at Berlin I got Mr Smith to draft a letter to invite tenders for the ship. On October 14th 1899 I received from him the complete specifications for the ship and engines, and on the 17th I received and approved the draft of a letter inviting tenders. The letter was sent to fourteen Firms, several draughtsmen were sent to No. 1 Savile Row to make tracings of the plans, but only two firms sent tenders. One from Barrow in Furness amounted to £90,000, another from the Dundee Ship Builders' Company, amounted to £66000.

Both these tenders were preposterous and quite out of the question. So I sent for Mr Paterson, the Managing Director of the Dundee Company and had a long conversation with him, to bring him to reason. Mr Smith also had a full discussion with him. The result was that on December 5th 1899 Mr Paterson agreed to a more reasonable tender; and on the 14th I accepted the Company's tender of £34,050 for the ship and £9700 for the engines. The Company immediately began to collect oak timber. No other Firm could either have got the timber together, or could have found shipwrights accustomed to wooden ship building. I had decided that the name of the ship should be the *Discovery*, an overseer named Mr Bate was appointed to watch every detail of the building and make weekly reports of progress, and on March 16th 1900 the keel was laid. Admiral Markham, as Secretary of the Ship Committee, received the weekly reports from Mr Bate, and passed them on to Mr Longhurst.

I then began to collect data from the Commander, when he should take charge, relating to the provisions, clothing, and sledge travelling. I received names of Firms and opinions respecting different kinds of preserved foods from Dr Nansen and others. On the 28th of March 1900 I had a small Committee, consisting of Admiral Markham, Dr Koettlitz and myself, and made progress in preparing the list of provisions. On April 5th I got Dr Mill to draw up a report on our meteorological instruments, and afterwards corresponded with the Antarctic authorities at Berlin with a view to arranging concerted action as regards observations.

In September the services of Scott and Royds became available; and they went through a course of magnetism with Captain Creak at Deptford. Royds, Barne, Armitage & Shackleton also went through a course at Kew. On October 8th Scott joined me in Norway. I introduced him to Dr Nansen and Dr Hjort, and on the 11th we went for a cruise in the *Michael Sars*. On the 17th we dined with Nansen at Lysaker. Scott arranged about ski, sledges, and cooking apparatus. On the 20th Scott went to Copenhagen to see about ordering pemmican. From the 21st to the 24th he was at Berlin and Potsdam, making the acquaintance of Baron Richthofen and Erik von Drygalski, and talking over the work of the two expeditions.

For the Arctic Expedition of 1875 Manuals were prepared at my suggestion, with Instructions and Information which would otherwise have to be collected from numerous sources. There were two, one on geography and ethnology edited by myself at the expense of the Council of the R.G.S.; and the other on other branches of science edited by Professor Rupert Jones and paid for by the Government.

I decided that a similar Antarctic Manual should be prepared containing like Instructions and Memoirs on the various branches of science; as well as the Antarctic parts of the voyages of Dumont D'Urville and Wilkes, and the journals of Biscoe and Balleny from manuscripts in the R.G.S. Library. Maps were prepared by Mr Batchelor under my superintendence. On November 21st 1900 I entrusted the work of editing the Manual to Mr George Murray, who thoroughly entered into the plan I

[21]

2. Cyril Longhurst – Secretary of the Expedition.

had sketched out, and went to work with a will. He secured the best contributors for each subject, and by July 1901 the Antarctic Manual was completed and distributed – a most valuable book.

On December 6th 1900 it was decided that the Royal Geographical Society should be the owner of the *Discovery*, and that I, as President, should be the Managing Owner. I wrote to the Dock Committee and obtained a promise that no charge would be made for the use of the dock when the ship came round to the Thames. Longhurst transacted all the business, and made all the arrangements with reference to insuring the ship from Dundee to Melbourne (Lyttleton).[14]

The House Flag was made at Dundee: the cross of St George at the hoist, the fly per fess argent arcd azure swallow tailed, over all the badge of the Society.

I also designed the sledge flags, on the same principle, for the officers, to be made by their mothers or wives; at the hoist the cross of St George, the fly of the colours of the arms swallow tailed, with a bordure of the same, over all the crest on principal charge. They were like the sledge flags I designed for the officers of the 1875 Arctic Expedition. Each has a motto.

ANTARCTIC MANUAL

Contents of the Manual

3. George Murray F.R.S.
Editor of the Antarctic Manual.

Three Antarctic maps with tracks of explorers, drawn by Mr
Batchelor, under the superintendence of Sir Clements
Markham; in a pocket.

VIII

The Executive Work
SECOND PERIOD

26 Nov. 1900 to 31 July 1901

8 months

Before handing over charge to Captain Scott it was absolutely
necessary to get rid of the useless Joint Committees, some
account of which will be given in an Appendix. I had suffered
almost intolerable worry and annoyance from them during the
whole time that I had been in charge of the executive work. It
was certain that the expedition could never be ready to start
unless Scott was given a free hand. The nuisance *must* be abated.

After consultations with me, Scott drew up an excellent
scheme for the future conduct of the work. He prepared a

preliminary estimate of the whole cost divided into 6 Heads, each with Sub-heads, and leaving a balance for the expenses after the Expedition starts: the estimate was very carefully prepared, the Heads being as follows:—

My Estimate 1897		Scott's Estimate 1900	Actual cost 1902	Final 1903
35,000	1. Construction of the Hull of the Ship	£36,250	£38,624	
	2. Construction of Engines	£10,600	£11,634	
18,000	3. Wages and Salaries	£17,400	£11,014	
11,000	4. Provisions and Clothing	£ 9,150	£10,172	
6,000	5. Travelling and shore outfit	£ 4,780	£ 3,188	
2,000	6. Completion of Ship's furniture	£ 3,300	£ 3,851	
	Equipment expenses	£81,480	£78,779	
8,000	7. Expenses after starting (except wages)	£11,520	2,785	
		£93,000	£81,561	£83,187

Scott was to be empowered to incur expenditure up to the sums set down opposite the several Heads, altering the amounts for the Sub-heads at his discretion. His expenditure was to be controlled by a Joint Finance Committee consisting of the two Presidents and the two Treasurers or their representatives.

Scott's scheme was approved by a Resolution of the R.G.S. Council on November 26th 1900, and became law.

The Royal Society officials, instead of having their President on the Committee, saw fit to request the Treasury to nominate an official to take his place. That Department agreed to the arrangement, and appointed Mr Rt Chalmers C.B. The Finance Committee thus consisted of the R.G.S. President as Chairman, Mr Chalmers, Mr Kempe R.S. Treasurer, and Mr Somers Cocks R.G.S. Treasurer. We met first on December 12th 1900, and agreed to meet once a month in the R.G.S. Council Room, Captain Scott and Mr Longhurst being in attendance. Mr Chalmers is a strong man and an excellent financier, and leads the Two Treasurers. He is friendly to Scott and the Expedition provided that not a sixpence more is asked for from the Government. Agreement prevails, and it has proved a thoroughly efficient Committee.

Scott was now able to proceed, unhampered, with the preparations. The officers were actively employed. Armitage went to Norway about sledges and fur clothing. Mr Wilton was employed to get 22 Siberian dogs and bring them to this country. Royds went to Dundee; went to the summit of Ben Nevis in the dead of winter to see the system of meteorological registration; and went to Lerwick after men. Barne went through the magnetic course, and also to the summit of Ben Nevis. Shackleton also went through the magnetic course, and was very busily employed with the library and other details, and afterwards with the provisions, and hold stowage. Skelton was at Dundee nearly the whole time, overlooking the building of the engines, and he looked after the photographic arrangements. Koettlitz studied the phyto-plankton and bacteriology, and watched over the testing of the provisions. Wilson's work was connected with the vertebrate zoology. Hodgson went for an oceanographic cruise with Dr Hjort in the *Michael Sars*, on the Norwegian coast. All were busily employed.

Hitherto Scott and Longhurst had shared the room at 1 Savile Row, but it was much too small. So Mr Hughes (Sec. R.G.S.) took Scott to Lord Esher at the Board of Works to ask for accommodation in the London University building. They were courteously received, and two good sized rooms were assigned to the Expedition on the ground floor. 'National Antarctic Expedition' was written over them; with 'Commander' over one door and 'Secretary' over the other. Henceforward the address was 'University Building, Burlington Gardens, W.'

The *Discovery* was to be launched on the 21st of March 1901. Scott had been to Dundee at intervals: Skelton and Royds almost constantly. All had received the most cordial hospitality from Mr and Mrs George Baxter; whose kindness will long be remembered by them. Lady Markham launched the good ship and named her the *Discovery*. The Directors of the Company gave a luncheon afterwards at which there were speeches, and the Baxters gave a dinner party the same evening.

The ship had to receive her engines, and to be rigged before coming round to the Thames: Royds and Skelton remaining at Dundee to superintend. Sir Anthony Hoskins had obtained from the Admiralty a promise to supply the hemp cordage, anchors and cables at cost price.

Scott had an unprecedently difficult task before him. A young officer, with everything to learn, he showed a grasp of the general problem, as well as of all the intricate details which was most remarkable. He brought to the work a very able and capable mind, a sound and clear judgement, and an excellent memory. He showed unfailing tact and most conciliatory bearing, combined with firmness and resolution when necessary. He is an admirable organizer, a born leader of men, sympathetic, and full of forethought and anxiety to meet all the reasonable wishes of his gallant companions. Above all Scott has the instincts of a perfect gentleman.

The R.S. Joint Committee, of which more presently, added tenfold to his worries and anxieties. Its Hydrographic Clique had done all it could to destroy his reputation and prevent his appointment. Then, while Scott was fully occupied with all the multifarious work of the expedition, the united Professorial and Hydrographic Cliques of the Joint Committee combined to undermine his authority and indeed to wreck the expedition. Scott's position was not safe, and he was kept on the tenter hooks of anxiety until all the machinations of the enemy were thwarted and the storm was weathered, on April 26th 1901, by Pilot Goldie: but of this hereafter.

It was important that the base station of the Expedition should be at Lyttleton New Zealand, and not at Melbourne, for several reasons, but it was necessary that there should be a magnetic observatory at the base station. There was one at Melbourne, but none in New Zealand. I was anxious that a magnetic observatory should be in working order at Christ Church, New Zealand, in time for the Expedition to make Lyttleton its base station.

On March 30th 1901 I heard from Mr Glazebrook at Kew Observatory that the magnetic instruments were ready for despatch to New Zealand. Subsequently, I received full assurances from the Honble C. C. Bowen, and from the magnetician at Christ Church, Mr Coleridge Farr, that the observatory had been built, and the instruments had arrived; so that all would be in working order long before the *Discovery* could be there. Thus the Expedition would have a more suitable base station, in a better climate, and 500 miles nearer its work.

The Siberian dogs too, which went out in charge of a man named Weller, in July, will be in a better climate and will be better looked after in New Zealand, than at Melbourne.

The trial trip of the *Discovery* took place, outside the Tay, on May 14th and was very satisfactory. Her steering qualities were found to be excellent, and she went 8.8 knots under steam.

On the 17th King Edward VII became Patron of the Antarctic Expedition at my request, at the same time expressing an intention to visit the ship before she starts on her voyage. On the 18th Mr Longstaff subscribed £5000 for a second ship on the condition that the fund was under the sole management of the R.G.S. Council. Mr Thomasson subscribed £500.

At the R.G.S. Anniversary, on May 20th 1901, I dwelt on the position and progress of the Expedition in my Address, and on the urgent necessity for a second ship. By this time Pilot Goldie had twisted the professorial tails and all danger from their machinations was at an end. I was, therefore, able to announce that the Councils of the two Societies were in complete accord. At the R.G.S. Anniversary dinner all the Antarctic officers were our guests. The Lord Chief Justice was on my right, and Lord Mansfield (Barne's cousin) on my left. Scott returned thanks for the toast of the evening 'Success to the *Discovery*.'

The ship had her engine and boiler on board, built by Messrs Gourlay, her auxiliary engines, and was fully rigged. Skelton spoke highly of the engines, there was condensing machinery in the engine room, and a well fitted up work shop on the port side. In the first days of June the ship was to go round to the Thames.

I went up to Dundee and was most hospitably received by the Baxters, where Scott was also staying. On May 29th the rudder was got up and down. On the 30th the spanker boom was rigged as a derrick over the screw well, with an iron hook and pulley, and a purchase to raise the propeller. Mr Smith and I were present, as well as Mr Paterson and Mr Kidd the Company's Secretary. When the propeller was nearly up, the iron hook parted, and the propeller went down by the run. Scott had a very narrow escape from the pulley falling on his head. It was necessary to go into dry dock, to ascertain what damage had been done. But the hook had never been tested, and Mr Smith advised that £250 should be kept back until all the iron had been tested, in accordance with the agreement.

On May 31st Mr Kidd delivered to me the Builder's Certificate, and Longhurst got the ship registered at the London custom house. She was to sail under the Merchant Shipping Act. The King had approved of her flying the white ensign, but the Secretary to the Admiralty objected. So it became desirable that Scott should belong to some yacht Club. I wrote to Sir Cuthbert Quilter Vice Commodore, and Captn Pretyman Rear Commodore, and he was elected a member of the Harwich Yacht Club, to fly the blue ensign, and a blue burgee with a yellow lion rampant.

The Company were very prompt in repairing the damage, and the *Discovery* left Dundee on the 3d of June 1901, accompanied by the Baxters and many other friends as far as Broughty Ferry. It was lovely weather. The mess consisted of

    1. Sir Clements Markham, Prest R.G.S., K.C.B.
    2. Commander Robert F. Scott R.N., F.R.G.S.

3. Lieutenant Armitage R.N.R.
4. Lieutenant Royds R.N., F.R.G.S.
5. Lieutenant Shackleton R.N.R., F.R.G.S.
6. Mr Reginald Skelton R.N.
7. Mr George Murray F.R.S.
8. Mr Hodgson

On the night of the 5th a leak was discovered under the engine room, due I believe to something having been started when the accident happened to the propeller.

We entered the Thames early in the morning of June 6th 1901 and in passing the *Worcester* the cadets manned the rigging and gave us three tremendous cheers. By 2 P.M. the *Discovery* was secured in the East India Export Dock behind the Blackwall Railway Station. The dock Committee provided a large shed to deposit stores and provisions.

The work of getting coals on board, and stowing the holds then proceeded rapidly. Charlie Royds, as First Lieutenant, worked like a dragon from early dawn to late. As the leak continued the ship went into Mr Green's dry dock from July 6th to 10th. Some additional caulking was done, but the mystery was not solved. On the 10th she returned to the East India Dock; Mr Smith and Mr Bate declaring that a certain amount of water always made in a wooden ship, that people accustomed to water tight steel ships forgot this; and that the leak was trifling, causing neither danger nor discomfort. But it is a source of anxiety. The ship had been commissioned and the men joined on July 1st.

Among additional appliances electric light was supplied and a large metal wind mill for working one of the dynamos. It is the invention of Mr Arthur Bergtheil, of the firm of Messrs Bergtheil and Young. Sir Joseph Hooker had strongly advised the provision of a captive balloon, and Scott was anxious to be supplied with one. He wrote to the *Times* appealing for a special subscription for a balloon of sufficient dimensions to carry a single observer to the height of 500? feet. Such an ascent, on a clear day, might yield not only geographical discovery, but information of immense importance to the plans and safety of the expedition. He believed that the experiment was worthy of trial. Scott received £80 towards it at once, and £500 came in afterwards, being due to Longhurst's exertions. The cost charged by the War Department for a balloon and gas stored in cylinders sufficient for 4 or 5 ascents, was £1380. The Finance Committee resolved to make another Sub-head for this sum. Mr

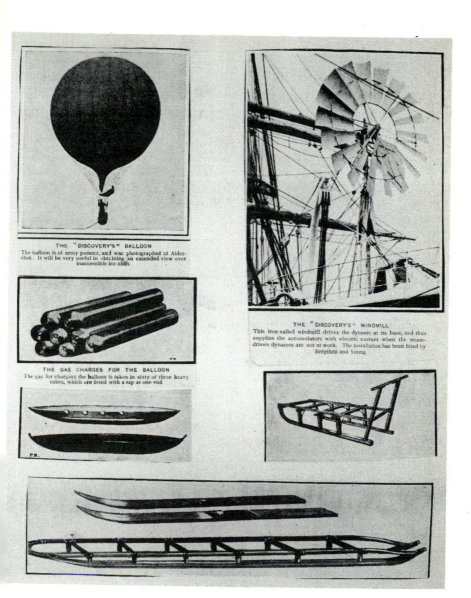

THE "DISCOVERY'S" BALLOON
The balloon is of army pattern, and was photographed at Aldershot. It will be very useful in obtaining an extended view over inaccessible ice cliffs

THE GAS CHARGES FOR THE BALLOON
The gas for charging the balloon is taken in sixty of these heavy tubes, which are fitted with a tap at one end

THE "DISCOVERY'S" WINDMILL
This iron-sailed windmill drives the dynamo at its base, and thus supplies the accumulators with electric current when the steam-driven dynamos are not at work. The installation has been fitted by Bergtheil and Young

4. Antarctic equipment.

Skelton, Mr Shackleton, Heald a seaman, and Lashly a stoker went to Aldershot and were instructed in the art of filling and working a balloon; and the 60 gas cylinders became conspicuous objects on the upper deck of the *Discovery*. The balloon, of gold beater's skin, has a capacity of 800 cubic feet.

Great crowds came to see the *Discovery* in the East India Dock. The relations were frequently on board, and it was most interesting and rather pathetic to see them finding great consolation in furnishing and arranging the cabins. Scott had his dear old Mother, and his sisters Mrs Macartney, Mrs Campbell, Mrs Brownlow, and Miss Scott. Charlie Royds had his mother and two sisters. Barne had his mother Lady Constance and a sister. Shackleton had his fiancée and her two sisters. Dr Koettlitz and Dr Wilson had their wives. Mrs Armitage was near her confinement, Mr Longstaff and I having been asked to be godfathers. The library was got on board and arranged, and a catalogue was printed. Two pianos were presented, and a pianola by Mrs Baxter. All the games were given by Mrs Longstaff. The crockery and glass had on them a design prepared at my request by Mr Reeves, a penguin surrounded by a scroll with the name of the ship &c. Shackleton got a type writer, make up box, and dresses, and learnt conjuring. I supplied a Commemoration Book with birthdays and great events.

On July 3d 1901 the Geographical Club gave a farewell dinner to the Antarctic officers at the Ship Inn, Greenwich. A special steamer took the party down the river and back. I took the chair, with Scott and George Murray on either side. Dr Keltie was opposite to me, with Armitage and Royds on either side. All the Royal Society officials were invited, but only one came, Mr Kempe the Treasurer. We mourned the loss of Sir Anthony Hoskins who had done so much for the Expedition; but my old messmate Sir Vesey Hamilton was with us, and Mr Longstaff. All the Antarctic Officers were present, and it was an unusually large gathering. We toasted and Royds sang; and it was a grand success. I proposed the healths of Scott, and of the officers, of Mr Longstaff, and of Captain Creak our great magnetic authority. Scott did a very graceful thing in proposing the health of young Longhurst, with whom, he said, he had worked so pleasantly for nearly a year, and whose services had been so valuable to the Expedition.

On July 16th 1901 the Bishop of London, complying with a request, but most willingly and with hearty good will, came on

5. The bridge and forecastle of *Discovery* from the main topsail.

board the *Discovery* to address the officers and men of the Antarctic Expedition. It was a very impressive scene. The officers and men occupied the space between the hatchway and the main mast, with relations behind. The Bishop came up from below in his robes, preceded by his Chaplain holding the crozier. It was a beautiful address and evidently considered with care. He touched upon the greatness of the enterprise, upon its dangers and hardships; but he did not dwell long on this side of the subject. He rather impressed upon his audience the need for a serious and thoughtful habit of mind during such a service, never to forget that God is always with them. Above all he spoke of the necessity of good comradeship, of sympathy for each other, and tenderness for failings and shortcomings. At the blessing he took the crozier and held up his hands. None could have failed to be impressed. The Bishop presented a bible and prayer book, with inscriptions, to be used for divine service. I afterwards asked him to write a prayer for daily use, which he promised to do. Scott had made the same request. It is as follows:

> Oh Almighty God, who hast appointed all things in heaven and earth in a wonderful order, be pleased to receive into thy most gracious protection the men who sail upon the ship *Discovery*. Grant that their labours may show forth thy praise and increase our knowledge. Preserve them in all danger of body and soul, nourish them in one spirit of godly unity and high devotion and bring them home, Oh Father, in love and safety, through Jesus Christ our Lord.
>
> Amen.

The text of the Bishop's address was 'Behold how good and how pleasant it is for brethren to dwell together in unity.' Ps cxxxiii.1.

The Hymns sung by the men, led by Charlie Royds, were 540, 'Fight the good fight', 165 'Lord thou hast been our refuge from one generation to another', and 370 'Eternal Father strong to save.'

In the last two meetings of the Finance Committee when Scott was present, great progress was made with the accounts; which were intricate. A Clerk from the Treasury had conducted an audit, & all was put straight. Longhurst's petty cash account was always in apple pie order; and at the last meeting but one, Scott bore witness to the great value of Longhurst's services and requested the Committee to recognize them in some substantial way. A sum was at once granted to the Secretary in addition to his salary (£50).

The ship sailed under the Merchant Shipping Act. Scott had to receive a Certificate; and all on board signed articles. The Accountant General of the Navy obligingly undertook to make all the arrangements about the allotments, both as regards the Expedition and the Naval pay of the men.

I drafted an almost identical letter of appointment to all the officers and members of the scientific staff, which was sent to them before the ship left the dock, signed by the two Presidents.

At last all was ready, three years provisions were stored on board, and 300 tons of coal. But the ship was remarkably buoyant, drawing only 15.4 forward and 17 aft. She only came down 1 inch in the water for every 11 tons.

It was a fitting ship for that gallant company, the strongest ship ever built for ice work in this country, and the best adapted for scientific work, a suitable command for such a leader. A close intimacy of over a year more than fully confirmed all I thought of Scott's qualifications. I see in him:

'The reason firm, the temperate will
Endurance, foresight, strength, and skill.'

IX

The Departure

The *Discovery* left the East India Dock at noon on July 31st 1901. A crowd of several hundred people at the dock gate, gave three hearty cheers. A goodly company was on board, to be landed at Greenhithe. First and foremost there was Sir George Goldie, 'the pilot who weathered the storm', and saved the expedition from being wrecked by irrational professors and hydrographers. There were Mr and Lady Vere Hughes, Dr Keltie and Mr Heawood, the R.G.S. Secretary and Librarian. Our Secretary young Cyril Longhurst, Lady Markham and all the relations. The training ships manned the rigging and cheered, having a boy on each truck. Captain Wilson-Barker of the *Worcester* provided boats at Greenhithe, and, after many warm hand shakes and farewells, the numerous visitors left the ship.

I went on, with the ship, to receive my last impressions and have my last communion of thoughts. Right aft was the grating, a pleasant place of resort, with the head of the tiller just rising above it: on the starboard side a store room, on the port the

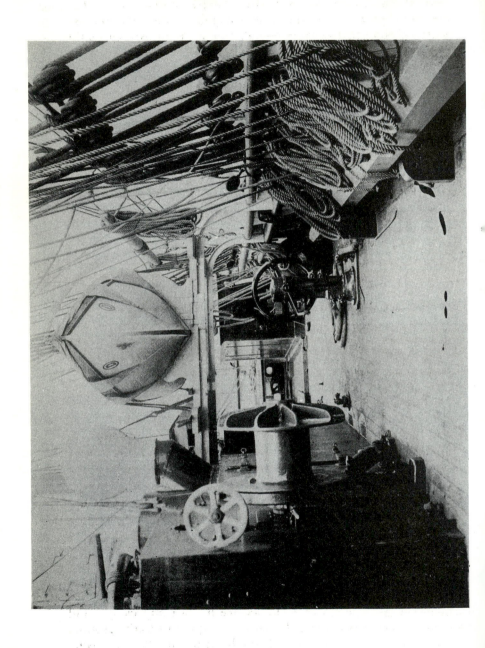

magazine and signal locker, amidships the wheel and screw well: then the hatchways of the boatswain's and carpenter's store rooms and mizen mast. The engine room hatchway on the port side and sky light, and auxiliary engine between the mizen and main mast. On the port side the boss of the spare screw, on the starboard the spare rudder with blades of the spare screw secured to it. Secured to the starboard combing of the engine room sky light is the great hook for raising the screw and a spare anchor. On the after skid beams, of iron, are two whalers and a dingey. Here also, and on the round houses aft the gas cylinders for the balloon are stowed. The mizen has a spanker and gaff topsail. The main has wire rigging – main course, double topsails, and a very square top gallant sail. There is a space between the main mast and the main hatchway where there will be divine service, but too small for a theatre. The drums for the dredging and sounding lines are against the fore part of the auxiliary engine house. Above are the fore skid beams of timber because of the magnetic observatory, built as strong as possible: as the 24 foot cutter is on them, as well as three whalers, one of them fitted for whaling: also some collapsible boats which are improvements on Berthan, some of Baron Toll's boats, and Nansen's canvas kayaks. The skids will also have to carry spars and timber for the huts.

Before the after hatchway the magnetic observatory is built amidships. It has a locker with cushions, and does not make a bad smoking room. On either hand, against the ship's side, are two laboratories fitted with shelves for bottles, and a flap table with small square window just above it, for microscope. In the one on the starboard side Hodgson and Dr Wilson will work at drawing, and preserving the organisms. Dr Koettlitz will have the laboratory on the port side.

The Bridge is over the magnetic observatory and laboratories, and is spacious with extensions forward on each side. It would have been an improvement if there had been extensions beyond the ships side. The officer of the watch should have a look out on each side, clear of the ship. A voice tube from the standard compass communicates with the wheel.

At the foot of the bridge ladder, on the starboard side, there are two dog kennels for an Aberdeen terrier puppy (Scamp) belonging to Scott, and a beautiful white Samoyed dog (Vinker) belonging to Armitage. There are also three kittens on board, a black and two Tabbies.

Before the magnetic observatory, with a passage between, is

the fore hatchway, then the fore mast, with hemp rigging, being within 30 feet of the magnetic instruments. Each hatchway has two doors, one to be closed before the other is opened, with a space between where all snow is to be brushed off the clothes.

Again the forecastle, on both sides and amidships, there are three petroleum cisterns and two right aft.

Under the forecastle is the second auxiliary engine and boiler on the starboard side. On the port side the sledges are stowed; and in the centre the bowsprit is stepped. On the forecastle are the windlass and anchors. The bowsprit is short and strong, with a jib, foretopmast, staysail and fore staysail. There are also main staysails and trysail. The crow's nest, for the main topgallant mast head, 4 ins longer than usual for Royds, is now stowed on the after skids.

Store rooms, engine room, and boiler occupy the after part of the ship nearly to the main mast which is in Scott's sitting room. There are four water tight compartments – the engine room, ward room, men's living deck, and galley.

The arrangements in the ward room and men's living deck compartments are shown in the plan. On the starboard side of the galley compartment is the sick bay with a bath and two berths, and the present use store room; on the starboard side Ferrar's cabin, the dark room for photographing, and the Physicist's laboratory. The galley is in the centre and table, with fresh water cistern and place for melting snow, and cupboards. Forward a store room and then the dead wood of the bows.

The cabins of the officers had been tastefully fitted up with pictures and other amenities by loving relations, and on some of their shelves were books of the Expedition library. Scott's sitting room has been charmingly arranged by his mother and sister. The piano is between Skelton's and Koettlitz's cabins, and the pianola between Hodgson's and Wilson's: there are to be pictures on the bulk heads of the Ward Room. One was up – Cook's old *Discovery* at Deptford.

The pantry is amidships. There is a slow combustion stove at each end of the ward room. A wooden funnel brings the cold fresh air down from the upper deck to the pantry floor, then through the stove to spread over the ward room deck as hot air, being taken away by an uptake at the after end. The same system of stoves, warming and ventilation, is applied to the men's deck.

Outside the ward room, on the starboard side, is the warrant officers' mess place for the assistant engineer, boatswain, carpenter, ship's steward, and cook. There are lockers round the

7. Deep sea sounding equipment on the side of
Discovery.

table, and three will sleep on them; the other two in the sick bay while unoccupied.

The rest of the men sling hammocks which are stowed, in the day time, in a pen on the port side forward. The lockers for their clothes &c form seats at meals and sofas for reclining or sleeping; and the tables, when not in use, are slung between the beams. Against the foremost bulkhead there is a bookcase with a library for the men. They also have a piano which Mr Else can play. Great attention will be given to the diet of the men, to their comfort, and to keeping the living deck dry.

The coal bunkers are on the port side of the engine room, and under the Ward Room. Then come the eight water tanks, which are of zinc, lined with wood, being within 30 feet of the magnetic observatory, with a hatchway at the after end of the men's deck, then the provision holds. The mess coming round was as follows:

1. Sir Clements Markham K.C.B. – Pres. R.G.S.
2. Commander Robt. F. Scott R.N. – F.R.G.S.
3. Lieut. A. B. Armitage R.N.R., J.R.G.S.
4. Lieut. Charles W. R. Royds R.N. – F.R.G.S.
5. Lieut. Michael Barne R.N.
6. Sub Lt. Ernest Shackleton R.N.R. – F.R.G.S.
7. Mr Reginald Skelton R.N.
8. Dr Koettlitz (Surgeon)
9. Mr Hodgson (Biologist)
10. Mr Ferrar (Geologist)
11. The dynamo man – Mr Bergtheil

I had much to examine and talk about, as we steamed along the south coast, with a smooth sea and beautiful weather. The *Discovery* anchored in Stokes Bay at 8 P.M. of August 1st 1901 near the pier, and remained there three days, the men having leave. The Commander in Chief, Sir C. Hotham, placed a steam pinnace at Scott's disposal.

Mrs Scott was staying with Captain and Mrs Egerton at Alverstoke. Her four daughters were at the Anglesea Hotel, also Shackleton's fiancée and her two sisters, and Mrs Wilson. Mrs Royds and her two daughters were on board Mr Yarrow's yacht astern of the *Discovery*. Lady Constance Barne and her daughter staid with Lord and Lady Hertford at Bembridge. Captain Robinson of the *Vernon* placed a steam pinnace at the disposal of the relations.

The indefatigable Secretary, Cyril Longhurst, arrived on

Friday, and on Saturday night we had to go through the Ship Builders' extra bill with Scott, Royds, and Skelton, which occupied us until 1.30 A.M.

On Sunday Captain and Mrs Egerton, Captain and Mrs Robinson, Lord Brassey, the Hertfords and others came on board, including Mr Tucker, son of the Master of the *Erebus*, who presented an engraving of Sir James Ross, and the barometer which was in Ross's cabin. Dr Wilson and Mr George Murray joined at Stokes Bay, and Admiral Markham arrived on Sunday evening and slept on board. Dr Mill also joined, who goes as far as Madeira to organize the physical and meteorological work. Mr Longstaff was established at the Marine Hotel, at Cowes.

On August 3d I placed the Instructions, signed by the two Presidents, in Scott's hands. They are practically the same as those I drafted in 1897.

On the morning of Monday, August 5th, the men all came back from their leave to their time, sober and respectable. The *Discovery* got under weigh, proceeded to Cowes, and made fast to a buoy near the *Osborne* at 10 A.M. Sir Henry Stephenson came on board about the King's visit. The officers were to be in caps frock coats and swords. His Majesty would be in Admiral's uniform. Mr Longstaff, Sir Leopold McClintock, and Sir Allen Young were to be on board; and in addition Sir Henry Stephenson said that the King would be glad to see Mrs Scott, and Admiral Markham. No one else was to be on board. The relations and Longhurst remained off, in the *Vernon*'s steam pinnace.

The King came from the *Osborne* with the Queen, the Princess Victoria, Sir Henry Stephenson, Sir Francis Knollys, Commodore Lambton, Miss Knollys and the Captain of the *Osborne*.

As His Majesty came over the side he called my name on seeing me, and I received the Queen, then kissed the King's hand as I had not seen him since his accession. He then told me to introduce him to Scott. Next I suggested Mr Longstaff being presented to him, and he approved. So I presented him, the King saying a few graceful words about his munificence, and introducing him to the Queen. His Majesty then had the officers presented to him by Scott, and he inspected the men. Mrs Scott was next presented, and the King shook hands with Sir Leopold McClintock, Sir Allen Young, and Admiral Markham.

The royal party went round the upper deck. The ward room and cabins, men's living deck and galley compartments were

[41]

then inspected in detail, the King and Queen showing great interest in all the arrangements. When the King came on deck again he talked to me about his sister who was then dying; also about the fine appearance of the men, and he expressed a high opinion of Scott's fitness. The men were drawn up on the starboard side.

His Majesty turned to Scott, took the case out of his pocket, and invested the Antarctic Commander with the Victorian order. It was a graceful act, intended to mark, in a very special way, the great interest taken by the King in the welfare of Scott and his gallant companions, and in the success of the great enterprise of which His Majesty is the Patron.

The King then made a speech to the officers and men. His Majesty said:

'Captain Scott, officers and men of the *Discovery* – I have had great pleasure in visiting this ship with the Queen, because of the interest I take in the Antarctic Expedition and its objects, and in order to wish you all God speed. You are going on a service from which, I believe, great results will accrue. I have often visited ships in order to say farewell when departing on warlike service; but you are starting on a mission of peace, and for the advance of knowledge. The results of your labours will be valuable not only to your country, but to the whole civilised world. I trust that you will be able to achieve the great work that is before you, and that you will all return safe and well.'

Their Majesties presented their portraits, with autographs, to the *Discovery*'s Ward Room. When they left the ship the explorers gave them three hearty cheers. The visit could not fail to impress both officers and men who received this gracious asurance that their labours would be appreciated by their King.

As soon as the royal party had returned to the *Osborne* the relations and Longhurst came on board again. Then came the leave taking during the afternoon. Longhurst and I had luncheon with Mr and Miss Longstaff at the Marine Hotel, where we remained during the afternoon, as there were accounts to go through. We went on board again at 6. There had been many visitors. Longhurst dined on board. Royds, Barne, and Armitage dined on board Mr Yarrow's yacht. Scott and I dined on board Allen Young's yacht to meet McClintock. Murray came rather later, and returned with us to the ship.

I came on board the *Discovery* at 11 P.M. to take a final farewell of my dear friends. I saw Koettlitz, Wilson, and Hodgson in their cabins, Skelton in the Ward Room. Scott, Armitage, Royds,

Barne, and Shackleton came to the gangway for a last farewell. Murray came in the boat. Longhurst and I slept at the Marine Hotel, and had breakfast with Mr and Miss Longstaff. Scott and Murray came on shore to breakfast. Scott went with us to the pier where the Portsmouth boat started, and there we waved our last farewell.

The *Discovery* left Cowes at 11.45 A.M. on August 6th 1901, and proceeded down channel. May all success attend the gallant explorers. They are engaged on a glorious enterprise; fighting no mortal foe, but the more terrible powers of nature arrayed against them.

Truly they form the vanguard of England's chivalry, and England's King gave them a farewell signal of good wishes from the *Osborne* as the brave ship steamed away. They will remember the words of their King, and the words of their Bishop, which will give them fresh vigour and renewed strength of purpose in their greatest difficulties.

> By mutual confidence and mutual aid
> Great deeds are done, and great discoveries made.
> The wise new prudence from the wise acquire
> And one brave hero fans another's fire.

X

Plan of Operations

Magnetic observations will be taken on board the *Discovery* on the passage out and, if time admits, the area of supposed greatest intensity south of Australia will be visited.[15] The ship will then proceed to Lyttelton, Christ Church being her magnetic base station, where instruments will be compared. Here she will take on the dogs and as much live stock as she can carry. During the voyage as much deep sea sounding and dredging will be done, as is compatible with making passages within given dates.

In December the *Discovery* will leave Lyttelton and shape a southerly course to the edge of the pack in about 170°E. There is reason, based on former experience, to hope that the pack will not cause any very long detention, and that open water to the south will be reached early in the navigable season. Ross entered the pack on January 5th in 171°50′E, and reached open water to the south on the 11th.

[43]

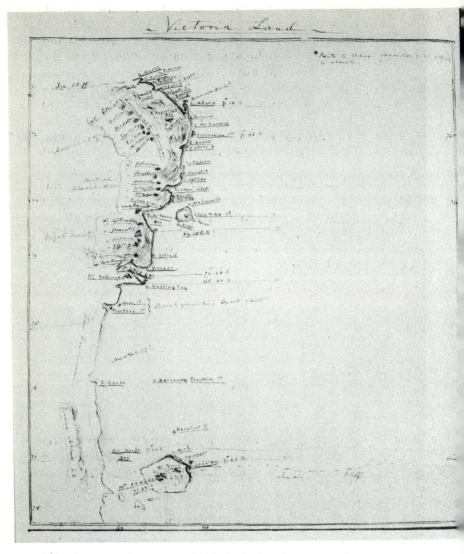

8. Victoria Land.

The *Discovery* would then proceed down the east coast of Victoria Land, from Cape Adare to Cape Crozier, perhaps leaving a cairn and record at some points arranged before hand. She will then proceed eastward along the ice cliff to Ross's furthest in 161°27'W. where the cliffs were much lower; but trending north of east. Here he saw mountains of great height with undulating outline, occupying 30° of the horizon. This was on February 23d 1842, in 78°11'S. Here is a crucial point. There was no pressure from the floe against the cliffs. If Scott finds it possible to force his way further east he will do so. It no doubt depends on the seasons. If he reaches the land which Ross thought he saw, it will be a great discovery; but he would probably have to winter in this entirely unknown region. Important discoveries will be made during the spring travelling. As the drift is N.W. he would probably be able to extricate the *Discovery* from the ice in the following navigable season. But there will be great risk.

In the effort to push eastward it will be one care to prevent the ship from being entangled in the drifting pack, for to have to pass a winter in it would mean the waste of a whole year. This may happen.

It may be that it will be found impossible to force a way to the eastward of Ross's furthest. In that case the rest of the navigable season can be devoted to an investigation of the ice cliffs, and possibly of the great ice mass of which they form the northern termination.

As soon as the formation of young ice gives warning that it is necessary, safe winter quarters will be sought, probably in McMurdo Bay. Here there is protection from the drift of ice; and an area of level shingle where the observatory huts will be set up. The observations during the winter will be:

Astronomical	Observation huts made by the Asbes-
Magnetic	tos Co. went out by P. and O. steamer
Meteorological	to Melbourne on Sept 5 1901. Cost
Pendulum	£100: plans and instructions for
Seismographic	putting them up taken out by Mr
Tidal	Bernacchi. 11ft. square, 9.8ft high
	(front) 7.4ft high (back).

and the scientific value of such series of observations will be very great.

The great object of the expedition is the exploration of the interior of Antarctic land. The discovery of a fossiliferous rock, even of a phanerogamous plant would be worth nearly the whole expenditure; far more a clearer knowledge of the general character of this unknown region. The sledge travelling is from September (the northern March) to December (June). At Wood Bay the sun is absent 94 days. This appears to be an excellent starting place. There is an ice foot to the south, round McMurdo Bay, to the volcanic region of Mount Erebus. Westward and inland there are no mountains visible from Mount Melbourne to Cape Gauss.

The whole force of the expedition must be concentrated on a great scheme of inland exploration. There may be three parties supported by depôts:

I.   one to strike inland to the westward,

II. another as far south as possible (along the Parry Mountains),

III. a third to explore the volcanic region. There may be much more formidable difficulties to overcome than are anticipated. It will be a great work needing a guiding head and close attention to details. We know our men, we know that their sledge flags will be borne far into the unknown, & if they do a tenth of what we hope to be possible it will be a great success.

In January the explorers will be cutting a way through the ice to bring the *Discovery* once more into open water. The navigable season of 1903 will see further geographical work done, and probably the 'Wilkes Land' problem will be solved. The ship will return to her base station at Lyttleton in April 1903; and will then cross the Pacific to Cape Horn, taking magnetic observations, and a series of deep sea soundings. Returning in August 1903 with a quarter achieved of what is hoped for and suggested, the Expedition will be a great success.

A second ship,[16] with relief and succour, should be ready to enter the pack in January 1903. If the *Discovery* has wintered at Wood or McMurdo Bay, she can be filled up with coals, provisions, and some live stock as soon as she gets clear of the land ice; and there will be two ships to conduct the work of the second navigable season.

But if Scott has been successful in pushing beyond Ross's furthest and has wintered in some unknown part of the eastern region, then the question of the proceedings of the second ship will be very difficult.

I found that the *Morgenen*, built by Svend Foyn at Tonsberg, was the strongest and best available ship. In September 1901 I went to Tonsberg to examine her, with Mr Bonnevie and Mr

Colbeck. Her price was 70,000K = £3880. I bought her on Oct. 31st for that sum, to be delivered at Sandefjord, to be docked and new boiler bed put in. Mr Bonnevie of Laurvik to be Agent. 451 tons [gross 437.26], 140 feet long [140], by 31 [31.4] by 16.7 [16.53]. 84 H.P. The two boilers built 1884, surveyed and retubed 1898, surveyed and tested 1900. Ship built at Tonsberg 1871, thoroughly caulked, rebolted and re-trenailed, and new green heart sheathing put on in 1900. Name the *Morning*.

Circulars and private letters were sent out, and every effort was made to raise the necessary funds. By Christmas £9000 raised; by Feb 14th £9500. The Prince of Wales subscribed £50. Feb 20 £10,000. The ship was brought across from Norway at Christmas, after some repairs, and was placed in the hands of Messrs. Green to refit.

Mr W. Colbeck R.N.R. to be Commander. I was elected Hon. Mem. of the Royal Corinthian Yacht Club, and the *Morning* became a yacht. On March 25th His Majesty the King subscribed £100, May 12. Mr Speyer £5000. The *Morning* sailed on July 8 and reached Lyttelton on Nov 16. She started for the Antarctic ice on Dec 6th with a mail for the *Discovery*, 300 tons of coal, 7000 lbs of fresh meat, and stores. Total subscribed £22,606: £1000 from the New Zealand Government. The *Morning* returned to Lyttelton, having relieved the *Discovery* and done her work, in March 1903.

THE INSTRUCTIONS

The Instructions for an exploring expedition ought to be written by one man, if they are to be clear, coherent, and intelligible. It would be an advantage if that one man was the Commander of the expedition himself, after he had made himself thoroughly conversant with the wishes and objects of his employers. It is folly to entrust such a duty to such a large heterogeneous Committee.

I drafted the Instructions for the Antarctic Expedition in 1897, making a few additions and alterations to bring them up to date in January 1901. This is the original draft which follows, and is practically the Instructions under which the Expedition sailed.

My Draft was mangled and rendered impossible by the Joint Committee.[17] Numerous verbal alterations were made with mischievous intent; and the main part, paragraphs 17 to 23, was cut out to give place to paragraphs (described elsewhere) which would have wrecked the expedition.

The matter had to be taken out of the incompetent hands of the Joint Committee; and was referred, for final settlement, by the two Councils, to a Select Committee of 6 able and competent men, one of them the highest living authority on polar subjects. The Select Committee restored my paragraphs at least in spirit, amplifying occasionally, and cut out most of the objectionable verbal alterations of the Joint Committee. One or two have been left which, though objectionable, are immaterial. Practically the Original Draft was restored. The Original Draft is here given in its purity, in one column; with any alterations or additions made by the Select Committee in the other.

Instructions
to the
Commander of
The Antarctic Expedition

1. The Royal Society and the Royal Geographical Society, with the assistance of His Majesty's Government, have fitted out an expedition for Antarctic discovery and exploration, and have entrusted you with the command.

2. The main objects of the expedition are to determine as far as possible the nature and extent of that portion of the South Polar lands which your ship is able to reach; and to make a magnetic survey in the southern regions to the south of the 40th parallel.

3. The Councils of the two Societies also attach importance to meteorological, oceanographic, geological, biological and physical investigations and researches.

The Joint Committee made a very mischievous alteration by making one paragraph of 2 and 3, to make it appear that *all* the objects mentioned in both paragraphs are of equal importance. The Select Committee should have restored 2 and 3. But they did not. They left out the word 'main', merely enumerated the objects in 2 and 3, and ended with 'neither of these objects is to be sacrificed to the other'. The meaning is neither of the two main objects: but the original paragraphs are spoilt: certainly not improved.

4. The Executive officers of the expedition, including yourself, belong to the naval service, and have been lent to the Societies by the Lords of the Admiralty. Their scientific work will be under your immediate control, and will include the magnetic and meteorological observations, the astronomical observations, the surveying and charting, and the sounding operations.

The scientific work of the Executive officers of the Expedition (the rest unaltered)

[49]

5. There will also be a civilian scientific staff over which there will be a Director with control and superintendence in all matters relating to the scientific duties of the gentlemen who have been appointed to assist him.

6. In all questions connected with the scientific conduct of the expedition you will consider the Director of the Civilian Staff as your colleague, and in all these matters you will observe such consideration in respect to his wishes and suggestions as may be consistent with a due regard to the instructions under which you are acting, to the safe navigation of the ship, and to the comfort, health, discipline, and efficiency of your crew. Those friendly relations and unreserved communications should be maintained between you which will tend so materially to the success of an expedition from which so many important results are looked for.

7. As the scientific objects of the expedition are manifold, some of them will come under the entire supervision of the Director of the Civilian Staff, others, such as the dredging operations, will depend for their success on the joint cooperation of the naval and civil elements; while many will demand the undivided

Associated with you, but under your command there will be &c.

I took paragraphs 6 and 7 from the Instructions of the *Challenger*.

Unaltered

attention of yourself and your officers. Upon the harmonious working and hearty co-operation of all must depend the result of the expedition as a whole.

8. You are to consider the magnetic survey as one of the two principal objects of the expedition. You will be supplied with a complete set of magnetic instruments, both for observations at sea and on shore, instructions have been drawn up for their use by Captain Creak R.N, and yourself and four of your officers have gone through courses of instruction at Deptford with Captain Creak or at Kew Observatory. The magnetic observatory on board the *Discovery* has been carefully constructed with a view to securing it from any proximity to steel or iron, and this has involved considerable expense and some sacrifice in other respects. We, therefore, impress upon you that the greatest importance is attached to the series of magnetic observations to be taken under your superintendence, and we desire that you will spare no pains to ensure their accuracy and continuity. The base station for your magnetic work will be at Christ Church (N.Z.) and that of the German Expedition will be at Kerguelen Island. The Govern-

'*The expedition*' will be supplied instead of 'you'. A piece of spite of the Joint Committee left as an eye sore by the Select Committee.

Unaltered

[51]

ment of the Argentine Republic has undertaken to establish a magnetic observatory at Staten Island. Your secondary base station will be at your Winter Quarters. You should endeavour to carry the magnetic survey from the Cape to Christ Church (N.Z.) south of the 40th parallel, and from Christ Church across the Pacific to the Meridian of Greenwich. It is also desired that you should observe along the track of Ross in order to ascertain the magnetic changes that have taken place in the interval between the two voyages. Observations are also to be taken as far south as possible, namely at your winter quarters.

Unaltered

9. The other primary object of the expedition is geographical discovery and exploration by sea and land, in the two quadrants of the four into which the Antarctic Regions are divided for purposes of reference, the Victoria and Ross Quadrants. It is desired that the extent of continental land should be ascertained by following the coast lines, that the depth and nature of the ice cap should be discovered, as well as the nature of the volcanic region, of the mountain ranges, and especially of any underlying fossiliferous rocks.

'Primary' object left out

Unaltered

10. A German expedition will start at the same time as the

Discovery, and there is to be cordial co-operation between the two expeditions as regards magnetic and meteorological observations, and in all other matters if opportunities offer for such co-operation. It is understood that the German expedition will establish an observatory on Kerguelen Island, and will then proceed to explore the Enderby Quadrant, probably shaping a course south between the 70°E and 80°E meridians, with the object of wintering, on the western side of Victoria Land, whence exploring sledge parties will be sent inland.

Unaltered

Unaltered

11. [A Swedish expedition will undertake the Weddell Quadrant, and will probably establish a winter station on the eastern side of Graham Island.]

Omitted as the necessary funds had not been raised as reported. But actually the Swedish vessel did start in Oct 1901.

12. You will see that the meteorological observations are regularly taken every two hours and, in accordance with a suggestion from the Berlin Committee, every day, at Greenwich noon. It is very desirable that there should, if possible, be a series of meteorological observations to the south of the 74th parallel.

Unaltered

Unaltered

13. Whenever it is possible, while at sea, deep sea soundings should be taken, with serial temperatures, and samples of sea water at various

depths are to be obtained, for physical and chemical analysis. Dredging operations are to be carried on ∧ whenever the circumstances are favourable.

∧ 'as frequently as possible' certainly not an improvement on 'whenever circumstances are favourable'

14. Instructions will be supplied for the various scientific observations; and the officers of the expedition will be furnished with a Manual on similar lines and with the same objects as the Manual supplied to the Arctic Expedition of 1875.

Unaltered

15. On leaving this country you are to proceed to Lyttleton, touching at any port or ports on the way that you may consider it necessary or desirable to visit for supplies or repairs. Lyttleton will be your base station. You will there fill up with live stock and other necessaries; and you will leave the port with three years provisions on board, and fully supplied for wintering, and for sledge travelling.

Unaltered

16. You are to proceed at once to the edge of the pack and to force your vessel through it, to the open water to the south. The pack is supposed to be closer in December than it has been found to be later in the season. But this depends rather on its position than on the time; and the great difference between a steamer and a sailing vessel perhaps makes up for any difference

Unaltered

[54]

in the condition of the pack.

17. On reaching the south water it will be for you to consider whether you will first examine the coast from Wood Bay to McMurdo Bay, with a view to finding a suitable place for landing or for winter quarters; or whether you will endeavour to proceed at once to the most eastern point reached by Sir James Ross in 1842, along the ice barrier, with the object of prosecuting further discoveries. The region to the eastward of this point is entirely unknown. An advance in this direction to decide the eastward extension of the ice cliff, and to discover the land believed to exist in the Ross Quadrant, to the south of the Pacific, will be of the highest importance.

18. Equal importance attaches to a complete examination of the ice mass which ends in the cliffs discovered by Sir James Ross; to an exploration of the volcanic region of Mount Erebus, and to a journey westward of McMurdo Bay.

19. This work includes one of the main objects of the expedition. Its geographical and geological importance cannot be over-estimated, and we have already alluded to the desirability of wintering in a high latitude, in the

'You are at liberty to devote to exploration the earlier portion of the navigable season; but such exploration should, if possible, include an examination of the coast from Cape Johnson to Cape Crozier, with a view to finding a safe and suitable place for the operations of landing in the event of your deciding that the ship shall not winter in the ice'. (This is supposed to please the Royal Society!)

Nearly the same

Nearly the same

unfortunately omitted

interests of magnetism and meteorology.

20. It will be for you to decide on the spot whether suitable winter quarters can be found for the ship, or whether you will put a small landing party on shore, and return with the ship. You are at liberty to take either course; bearing in mind that the very limited means of a landing party would be quite inadequate to secure the results we desire. This would require the whole force of the expedition working on a carefully planned and extensive system of sledge travelling.

'Owing to our very imperfect knowledge of the conditions which prevail in the Antarctic seas, we cannot pronounce definitely whether it will be necessary for the ship to make her way out of the ice before the winter sets in, or whether she should winter in the Antarctic Regions. It is for you to decide on this important question after a careful consideration of the local conditions. If you should decide that the ship shall winter in the ice, the following instructions are to be observed:— namely details about sledging operations &c from information which I supplied. In case of not wintering a party to be landed under the command of such person as you may appoint. No person to be left without his consent in writing, which you will be careful to obtain & preserve.'

21. Lieut. Armitage R.N.R. has been appointed navigator to the expedition. This officer has had (great) experience in the work of taking astronomical, magnetic, and meteorological observations during three polar winters. He has also acquired great experience in sledge travelling, and in the driving and management of dogs. You will, no doubt, find his knowledge

The Joint Committee thought they could detract from the merits of Armitage by scratching out the word great.

Unaltered

[56]

and experience of great use.

22. In the event of wintering, you will probably return to Lyttleton in March 1903, and to this country in August of the same year.

23. If adverse circumstances should hinder your advance and the accomplishment of our wishes in the above directions, there is an alternative route for discoveries westward from Cape North of Victoria Land, and another between the meridians of 110° and 160°E.

Unfortunately, so altered as to leave no instructions about a second navigable season. A useless paragraph substituted.

24. (In the event of an accident to the ship or of her detention) you should have left full details of your intentions with regard to the places where you will deposit records, and the course you will adopt, as well as particulars of your arrangements for the possible need of retreat, (to be forwarded to us from Lyttleton) so that in case of accident to the ship or detention we shall be able to use our best endeavours to carry out your wishes in this respect (and to raise such funds as may be necessary).

Unaltered

Omitted

Omitted

25. In an enterprise the nature of which we have explained to you, much must be left to the discretion and judgment of the commanding officer, and we fully confide in your combined energy and prudence for the successful issue of a voyage

Unaltered

which will engross the attention of scientific men
throughout the civilized
world. At the same time we
desire you constantly to bear
in mind our anxiety for the
health, comfort and safety of
the officers and men en-
trusted to your care.

26. While employed on this
service you are to take every
opportunity of acquainting us
with your progress and your
requirements.

Unaltered

27. Before the final return of
the expedition you are to
demand from the officers the
logs and journals they have
kept, and the charts, drawings, observations and collections that have been made.
These are to be sealed up and
disposed of as the Councils of
the two Societies may determine.

A gruesome paragraph about
successions to the command
in the event of fatalities
inserted.

Made fuller but not im-
proved.

'You and other members of
the expedition will not be at
liberty, without our consent,
to make any communications
to the press on matters relating to the affairs of the
expedition, nor to publish
independent narratives, until
6 *months* after the issue of the
official narrative.

28. The *Discovery* will sail
under the Merchant Ship-
ping Act, and it will be your
duty to see that all the
regulations of the Board of
Trade are complied with, and
that all on board sign articles
in accordance with the rules
of that Department.

Nearly the same

29. The ship will be owned by
the Royal Geographical Soci-

ety, and its President will be registered as her Manager, in pursuance of the requirement of the Act of Parliament.

30. The *Discovery* is the first ship that has ever been built expressly for scientific purposes in this kingdom. It is an honour to receive the command of her; but we are impressed with the difficulty of the enterprise which has been entrusted to you, and with the serious character of your responsibilities. The Expedition is an undertaking of national importance, and science cannot fail to benefit from the efforts of (yourself and of those under your orders.) You may rely upon our support on all occasions, and we feel assured that all on board the *Discovery* will do their utmost to further the objects of the Expedition.

Unaltered

'those engaged in it' *another piece of spite of the Joint Committee*: substituted for 'under your orders'.

ANTARCTIC SHIP *DISCOVERY*

Managing Owner, Sir Clements Markham K.C.B.
Owner, R.G.S.
Specially built for Antarctic work at Dundee by Dundee Ship Builder's Company.
Designed by Mr W. E. Smith, Chief Constructor.

	Dates
1899 April 17	Plans submitted to Sir Clements Markham.
1899 Dec 6	Mr Paterson, Managing Director, after sending in a tender for £66,000, agreed to one of £34,050 for the ship, and £10,322 for engines.

9. Antarctic ship *Discovery*.

1899 Dec 14		Sir Clements Markham accepted this tender.
1900 March 16		Keel laid. Mr Bate our Overseer.[18]
1900 Dec 6		Royal Geographical Society to be Owner. Sir Clements Markham Managing Owner.
1901 March 21		Lady Markham named and launched the *Discovery*.
1901 June 3		*Discovery* left Dundee.
1901 June 6–July 31 (55 days)		In East India Dock.
1901 Aug 1–Aug 5		In Stokes Bay.
1901 Aug 5		The King's visit at Cowes.
1901 Aug 6		Started from Cowes at noon.
1901 Aug 15		Funchal, Madeira. (Dr Mill came home from Madeira). Voyage of 58 days.
52 days {	Oct 8	*Discovery* arrived at the Cape, left Oct. 14th (George Murray came home Nov 2).
	Nov 29	*Discovery* arrived at Lyttleton.
	Dec 24	*Discovery* left New Zealand.

Report on the ship during the Atlantic voyage

If close hauled to the wind the ship makes excessive leeway. She was kept about 7 points off, and even then she sagged away nearly a point. The ship must be accounted a poor sailer, and cannot be expected to beat to windward, though she might make a reasonably good passage under sail, with a fair wind.

The ship has leaked considerably. The provision cases were stowed close down to the keelson in the fore and main holds. The water which got into the ship, having no space in which to collect, rapidly rose amongst the cases to a height of 2 feet. The holds were cleared, and proper floors constructed with an amply sufficient bilge space beneath. The damage to the submerged cases was comparatively slight, and the restoring was so satisfactorily done that, despite a considerable reduction of space, the provisions were easily stowed in their original holds. Improvements in the pumping arrangements were also carried into effect.

In a fresh breeze, with a heavy sea, the ship proves very stiff, and an excellent and most comfortable sea boat. She has, on the whole, done as well as could be expected, for a vessel of her type.

'The ship is good in every respect except she wants a gale to move her' (Royds). 'It will be a mighty strong wind before we have to shorten sail.'

Coal consumption

The most serious matter is the expenditure of coal.

Coal on board on leaving London............................... 245 tons
Coal received at Madeira 55
                                                                        ——
                                                                        299
                                                                         63
                                                                        ——

Coal expended for distilling   16 ⎫
          cooking   3 ⎪
          electric light   5 ⎬ 58 days
          lighting up boilers   9 ⎪
          remaining   30 ⎭
                                                         ——
                                                         63
                                                        ====

Therefore coal actually expended in propelling the ship 236. Actual number of days under steam 33, a consumption of 7 tons a day. Probably there would be a much more economical result if the ship was run at 5 knots instead of 6½. But the economy of the engines is less than was hoped for, and the necessity for nursing the coal is proportionately increased.

Magnetic Observations

The magnetic observations will be in connection with series taken, in co-operation, at several observatories, namely

1	Kew	7	Staten Island
2	Falmouth	8	Kerguelen Island
3	Bombay	9	English Expedition
4	Mauritius	10	German Expedition
5	Melbourne	11	Potsdam
6	Christ Church N.Z.	12	Swedish Expedition

The object is to achieve a series of synoptic charts which will allow of the variations in the magnetic condition of the whole earth being traced in detail during a definite period, and so to provide the necessary basis from which alone the fundamental problems of terrestrial magnetism can be more clearly approached. The observing stations to take part in this International Co-operation are distributed over the globe with a uniformity never hitherto attained.

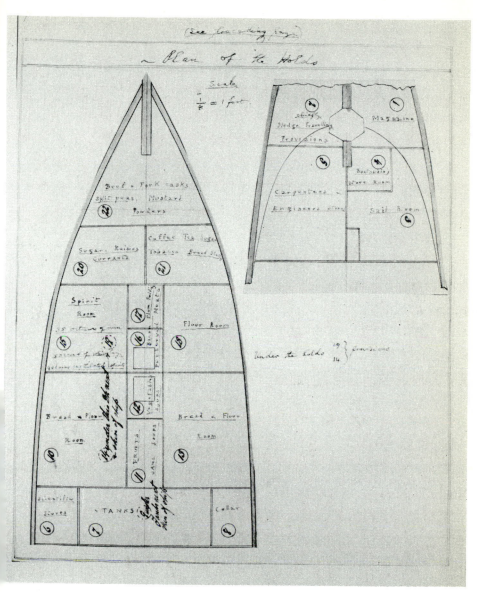

10. Plan of the holds.

The observations will be of two classes – of the three elements at intervals of an hour on certain terminal days; so as to obtain a comprehensive view of the diurnal variations of terrestrial magnetism:– and of the three elements during one specified hour on each term day; to trace the course of individual disturbances.

The *Discovery*, the *Gauss*, and all the observatories are supplied with identical forms for term days and term hours.

Declination
Horizontal Force
Vertical Force

All observations of the International Scheme will be made according to Greenwich Mean Time. On term days, two in each month, there will be simultaneous observations at each complete hour of the 24. At term hours there will be detailed observations during the hour. Printed forms are supplied for each, translated from those prepared by the German magneticians. The German Instructions have also been translated for the guidance of observers in the *Discovery*, and at our Observatories.

The magnetic observations on board the *Discovery* are in charge of the Navigator Lieut. Armitage, assisted by Lieut. Barne and Mr Bernacchi. They are the most carefully planned and completely thought out of all the branches of scientific work carried on by the expedition.

Meteorological Observations

The meteorology is in charge of Lieut. Charles Royds R.N. Observations are taken every two hours by the officers of the watch. A screen is fixed on the port laboratory, where there is always a current of air, on which there is a wet and dry bulb thermometer, a mercurial maximum, and a Sixe's maximum and minimum. The barometer, on the Kew pattern, is in the magnetic observatory, with its cistern about 12 feet above the water line, and a barograph is kept at work in one of the hatchways. A thermograph and a hair hygrograph are placed on the outer walls of the magnetic observatory. The three recording instruments are kept running to Greenwich time. The temperature readings are checked by means of an Assmann's Aspiration Psychrometer, and sling thermometers are also supplied for comparison.

Rainfall observations will be attempted with a marine rain

gauge and evaporator on Dr Black's pattern, on the top of the weather deck house aft.

Surface temperature of the sea is taken each time the other instruments are read. At noon the colour of the sea water is measured by means of Forel's Xanthometer.

In the Antarctic Regions special observations will be made on the conditions of the upper atmosphere, by means of a captive balloon. Large box kites of Hargreave's pattern will also be used, to which light aluminium meteorographs will be attached. Special instruments are taken out for use on shore, including spirit thermometers graduated as low as −90, special Stevenson screens, low reading thermographs, sunshine recorders, and earth thermometers; also a Dines pressure anemometer, and an anemograph. A photographic spectrometer will be used for observing the Aurora, and Professor Ramsay has supplied a crypton vacuum tube that the green line of that element may be compared with the similar line in the spectrum of the Aurora.

The oceanographic observations will include determinations of the density of surface water by means of the hydrometer, and also direct measurements of salinity by titration of sea water with a solution of silver nitrate. This Department is in charge of Sub-Lieut. Shackleton; and Lieut. Barne has charge of the deep sea temperatures.

The Sledge Flags

The Knights of Chivalry used flags (called standards) with the Cross of St. George always at the hoist. This was to denote that, whatever family the bearer may belong to, he is first and foremost an Englishman. The fly is divided per fess (horizontally) with the colours of the arms, the edge fringed or bordered of the colours of the arms alternating over all the crest or principal charge. Swallow tailed. Extreme length 3ft 2½in, from head to split of swallow tailed 2ft 2in. Cross of St. George 12 inches square, width of cross 1¾ in.

At my suggestion the officers of the 1875 Arctic Expedition adopted this form for their sledge flags, and I designed their flags.

Also at my suggestion the officers of the Antarctic Expedition continued the tradition, adopting the same form for their sledge flags, which I designed.

Officers

Robert F. Scott – *Commander*, R.N., M.V.O., F.R.G.S.
Albert B. Armitage *Navigator*, R.N.R.
Charles W. R. Royds *First Lieutenant*, R.N., F.R.G.S.
Michael Barne *Second Lieutenant*, R.N.
Ernest Shackleton *Third Lieutenant*, R.N.R., F.R.G.S., F.R.A.S.
Reginald Skelton *Engineer* R.N.
Reginald Koettlitz – *Surgeon*
Edward Wilson *Assistant Surgeon* Civilians

Warrant Officers

J. H. Dellbridge *Assistant Engineer* R.N. H.M.S. *Majestic*
Thomas Alfred Feather – *Boatswain* R.N. H.M.S. *Boscowen*
Frederick E. Dailey *Carpenter* R.N. H.M.S. *Ganges*

Leading Stokers

Arthur L. Quartly R.N.
Thomas Whitfield R.N.
William Lashly R.N.
William Page R.N.
Frank Plumley R.N. (joined at the Cape)
William Hubert (*Artificer*) *not R.N.*

Petty Officers

Edgar Evans R.N. H.M.S. *Majestic*
David S. Allan R.N. H.M.S. *Majestic*
William Smyth R.N. H.M.S. *St. Vincent*
Jacob Cross R.N.
William Macfarlane R.N.
Thomas Kennar R.N.

Able Seamen (naval)

Henry J. Baker R.N.
Charles T. Bonner R.N.
James W. Dell R.N.
William L. Heald R.N.
Arthur Pilbeam R.N.
William Peters R.N.
John W. Waterman R.N.
Frank Wilde R.N.
T. S. Williamson R.N.

George Beaver Croucher R.N.
Ernest Edward Mills Joyce R.N.
George Thomas Vince R.N. Joined at the Cape
James Crean (from *Ringarooma*)
Jesse Handsley R.N.

Royal Marines
  Arthur Henry Blissett R.M.
  Gilbert Scott R.M.

Idlers
  Lewis C. Bernacchi F.R.G.S. (*Physicist*)
  T. V. Hodgson (*Biologist*)
  H. T. Ferrar (*Geologist*)
  Edward Else (*Ship's Steward*)
  Sydney Roper (*Cook*)
  Charles Clark (*Cook's Mate*)
  Charles R. Ford R.N. (*Steward*) H.M.S. *Vernon*
  W. J. Weller (*in charge of dogs*)
  Albert C. Dowsett (*Domestic*)
  Job Clarke (*Ward Room Servant*)
  Horace L. Buckeridge (*Laboratory Assistant*) Joined at the Cape

Merchant Seamen
  James Duncan (*Shipwright*)
  Hugh Miller (*Sailmaker*)
  James Masterton from Dundee
  John Mardon from Brixham
  John Walker from Dundee A.B.
  Robert Sinclair (joined at the Cape)
  Henry R. Brett (*Cook*)
  Clarence Hare (*Clerk at 21*)

Ages

Average age 27; of officers 30, of petty officers 27, of seamen 23, of stokers 28, of merchant seamen 29. Oldest Dr Koettlitz aged 40, youngest Hare (Clerk) 21. Over 30 there are 11 (4 officers 7 men) between 25 and 30 there are 18, 7 aged 25, 5 aged 24, 8 aged 23, 2 aged 22, 1 aged 21.

[67]

June 9th 1900

Sir,

We have great pleasure in announcing your appointment, by the Councils of the Royal Society and the Royal Geographical Society, to command the National Antarctic Expedition.

The approval of the Lords Commissioners of the Admiralty had previously been received; and we have requested that your time may be allowed to count as service at sea, while so employed.

We have also requested their Lordships to allow your name to be placed on the books of the *President*, while going through a course of instruction at Kew, and otherwise making preparations for the expedition.

We take this opportunity of offering you our congratulations on assuming the conduct of an enterprise involving difficulties and responsibilities of no ordinary character, and of great national and scientific importance.

You will receive all the aid, encouragement, and advice that we can give you, and we feel confident that there will be nothing wanting on your part, to bring the enterprise to a successful issue.

> We have &c
> (signed)
> Lister (F.R.S.)
> Clements R. Markham (F.R.G.S.)

Lieut. Robert F. Scott R.N.

Scott's acceptance of the command

United Service Club
June 11th 1900

My Lord and Sir,

I have the honour to acknowledge your communication of June 9th, acquainting me with my appointment as Commander of the National Antarctic Expedition.

I am keenly alive to the great honour done to me in this selection, and sincerely hope that the trust reposed in me may be justified by my conduct of the enterprise, and by my earnest wish to further its great scientific aims.

I am grateful for your kindness in the applications you have made on my behalf to the Lords Commissioners of the Admiralty, and feel that whilst in your service I can confidently leave in your hands my interests in a profession to which I am devotedly attached.

I have &c
Robert F. Scott
Lieutenant R.N.

The Presidents of the Royal Society
and the Royal Geographical Society

Scott's services

1886 *Boadicea* (masted) *Mid* (Capt Church) 1¾1 years. 'Entirely to my satisfaction'

1886 *Liberty* (brig) *Mid* (S. T. Target) 1½ months

1886 *Monarch* (masted) *Mid* (Capt Church) 1 year. 'A promising young officer'

1887 *Rover* (masted) *Mid* (Capt Noel) 1 year. 'An intelligent and capable young officer'.

1888 *Spider* *Sub* (F. G. Foley) 1½ months

1888 *Amphion* (masted) *Sub* (Capt Hulton) 4 months

1888 *Caroline* (masted) *Sub* (W. Wiseman) 3 months

1889 *Amphion* (masted) *Lt* (Capt Hulton). 1¼ years. 'A most promising officer'.

1889 *Sharpshooter* *Lt* (W. J. Anton) 1½ months 'A good navigator, zealous & attentive'.

1890 *Vernon* *Lt*. (Capt Hall) 1¼ years 'To my entire satisfaction'.

1891 *Vulcan* *Lt T* (Capt Durnford) 1 year 'Of much value to the service, and most promising'.

1892 *Vulcan* *Lt T* (Capt Robinson) 2 months. 'A zealous and excellent officer'.

1893 *Defiance*[19] *Lt T* (H. B. Jackson) 1½ years. 'A very clever, able and zealous officer.'

1894 *Benbow* *Lt T* (Capt Rooke) 1 month

1896 *Empress of India* *Lt T* (Capt McCleod) 1 year. 'Very painstaking and attentive.'

1898 to Sept 1899 *Majestic* Torpedo Lieut (L. Battenburg, Capt Egerton) 2 years. 'Showed great zeal and judgment and to my entire satisfaction'

COMMANDER OF THE EXPEDITION

Robert Falcon Scott
(Sledge Traveller)

(West Country) born at Devonport June 6th 1868. *Age 33* in 1901, *40* in 1908. Entered the navy 1886. *Rover* Capt Noel, Training squadron. Won the cutter race at St. Kitts March 1st 1887. Lieutenant R.N. – 1889. Torpedo Lieut. *Majestic* 1898. Volunteered and selected June 5th 1899. Appointed April 6th 1900 by the Admiralty. Appointed April 18th 1900 by Joint Executive Committee. Appointed June 9th 1900 by the Presidents. Commander R.N. June 30th 1900. Magnetician. Pet name *CON.* R.N., M.V.O., F.R.G.S. On return C.V.O. Mother Mrs. Scott, 80 Queen's Road, Chelsea. 80 Royal Hospital Road, Chelsea. 56 Oakley Street, Chelsea. *Single.*

Sledge Journeys 94 days (880 miles). Reached 82.17.S. 2nd season 79 days. Over inland ice. Total travelling 197 days.

Expedition £41.13.4 a month = £500
Navy   365
                                   ——————
                                        865

SECOND IN COMMAND AND NAVIGATOR

Albert Borlase Armitage
(Sledge Traveller)

(Yorkshire) *born July 2d 1864.* Father a physician at Scarborough, then London. 1878 Cadet in the *Worcester* to 1880 (1st class extra). *Age 37.* Born in the Braes of Balquhidder, Perthshire, but a Yorkshireman. 1886 P and O Company's Service. 1894–97 Harmsworth Expedition. 1881 Apprenticed to Tyson & Sons trading to Calcutta and W. Indies. In sailing ships 4½ years. R. G. S. Murchison Award 5 June

11. Captain Robert Falcon Scott
the commander of the Expedition.

1899. Lieutenant R.N.R. Volunteered and selected 29 May 1900 (22 years good service). Wife 23 St. John's Road, Richmond, *then* 5 Cambridge Villas, Cambridge Park. Mother in law Mrs Pearce, 11 Avenue Road, Regent's Park. *Married*. Daughter born 25 Oct 1901 called Cicely Markham, baptized by the Bishop of London 18 Dec 1901.

Magnetician. Charge of the magnetic observations.

Navigator.

Sang a song at the entertainment on 11 Sept.

Armitage is splendid. Quite unperturbed whatever happens, he goes on his way without hurry or excitement, but with the most painstaking exactitude. Without any particular cleverness, he possesses one of the soundest judgments I ever met with. He is universally liked and respected on board.

'I like Captain Scott better than ever'. Armitage 10 Oct 1901.

Led the reconnaissance party to W. and the main Western Party – 54 days. *Total travelling* 91 days.

Expedition £450

Appointment of Charlie Royds

Sir

We have great pleasure in informing you that you have been appointed by the Councils of the Royal Society and the Royal Geographical Society, to be one of the executive officers of the Antarctic Expedition, serving under Lieut. Robert Scott R.N. who will be the Commander of the Expedition. Your appointment had previously been approved by the Lords Commissioners of the Admiralty.

A request has been made to the Admiralty that you may be borne on the books of the *President* with harbour time while

12. Albert Borlase Armitage
the second in command and Navigator.

preparing and fitting out; and that from the date of sailing you may be on full pay and your time counting as sea service. In addition you will receive £200 a year from the Antarctic Fund.

You have been a zealous volunteer for this important and difficult service; and we have confidence that the Commander will find in you a valuable colleague, and that you will do all in your power to ensure the success of the enterprise.

We have &c

Lister (P.R.S.)

Clements R. Markham (P.R.G.S.)

Lieut. Charles W. R. Royds R.N.
H.M.S. *Crescent.*

FIRST LIEUTENANT

Charles W. Rawson
Royds
(Sledge Traveller)

Rochdale (Lancashire) born *Feb 1st 1876.* Nephew of Wyatt Rawson. Cadet in the *Conway. Age 25½.* Training Squadron. Destroyer Squadron (Nore). H.M.S. *Crescent.* Volunteered and selected April 3d 1899. Appointed by the Admiralty April 6th 1900. Appointed by Exec Committee April 18th 1900. Lieutenant R.N. 31 Dec 1898. F.R.G.S. Pet name Charlie. Mother – Mrs Royds, Langston Lodge, Havant. *Single.* First Lieutenant, Charge of upper deck. Magnetician and meteorologist. Musician, Vocal and instrumental. Sang at the entertainments 13 Aug & 11 Sept.

A first rate seaman. The way in which he took charge of the meteorology, and the conscientious steady way in which he keeps the records, are alone enough to stamp him as a first class worker. He is an excellent officer and popular with the men; altogether the right man in the right place as First Lieutenant.

51 days sledge travelling on several trips. In the sledge reconnaissance to S.W. Sept 10. 2d season – journey over the ice barrier. *Total travelling* 104 days.

[74]

Expedition £12.10. a month	£150
Navy	£182
	£332

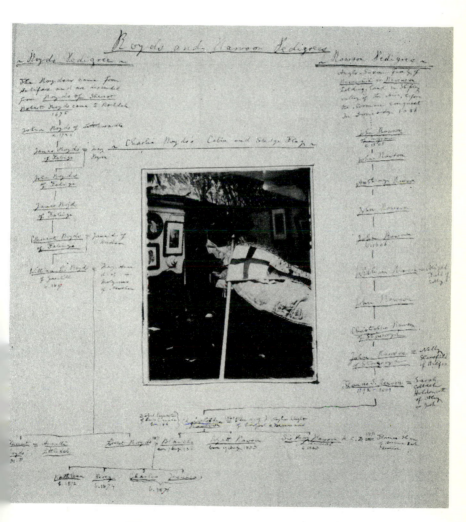

13. The pedigrees of Royds and Rawson,
drawn up by Markham.

14. Charlie Royds – the First Lieutenant.

15. Michael Barne – the Second Lieutenant.

Michael Barne
(Sledge Traveller)

(Suffolk) born at Beccles *Oct. 15th 1877.* Great Grandson of my old Admiral Sir George Seymour. *Age 24.* In 1908 – 31. Entered the navy 1893. *Majestic* then in China. Volunteered and selected June 5th 1900. Returned from China Jan 28th 1901. Lieutenant R.N. June 30 1900. Pet name Mik. Mother – the Lady Constance Barne, Satterley Park, Wangford, Suffolk, & Grey Friars, Dunwich, Saxmundham, Suffolk. *Single.* Magnetician and meteorologist. Chief Assistant to Armitage in magnetic observations. In charge of deep sea temperatures and all deep sea apparatus. Charge of ward room and domestics and main deck.

Barne is very popular all round, always ready to help any one, full of good humour, the most unselfish of mortals with moreover great undeveloped probabilities of performance; to be entirely trusted and given responsibility. He runs our mess, and is in charge of all the deep sea apparatus, which he does right well.

Commanded South Depôt Party 1902. S.W. Party 1903–04. *Total travelling 162 days.*

Expedition £12.10 a month	£150
Navy	£182
	£332

SUB-LIEUTENANT R.N.R.

Ernest Shackleton
(Sledge Traveller)

(Irish originally. Yorkshire, now Kildare) Born Feb 15th 1874. Father a Doctor at Norwood. *Age 27* in 1901, 34 in 1908, 35 in Feb 1909. 35 & 4 months 15 June 1909. 39 – 1913. In the merchant service from 1890. Sailing

16. Ernest Shackleton – the Third Lieutenant.

ships in the Pacific. The Castle line. Sub-Lieutenant R.N.R. Appointed Feb 17th 1901. R.N.R. – F.R.G.S. – F.R.A.S. Librarian. Conjuror. Stage Manager. Editor. *Engaged* 19 Wetherby Gardens. S. Kensington to Miss Dorman. In charge of holds, stores, and provisions. Magnetician. In charge of deep sea water analysis.

A marvel of intelligent energy. Besides keeping his watch, he has taken in hand all the holds, the issue and management of provisions, fixing the dietary and keeping all the books. He has taken over the examination of sea water with hydrometer and titration, and has obtained a thoroughly practical grasp of the whole thing; also the study of waves on Vaughan Cornish's plan. Never tired, always cheerful, he is exceedingly popular with every one. He also arranges the entertainments.

With Scott in his sledge journey to S. Nearly died of exhaustion. Invalided and came home in *Morning* 1903. Appointed Secretary to the Scottish Geographical Society 1904.

Expedition   £250

ENGINEER

Reginald Skelton
(Sledge Traveller)

(Norfolk) Born June 3d 1872 in Lincolnshire. *Age 29.* Engineer R.N. H.M.S. *Majestic* 1896. Appointed June 1st 1900. Father – Denver House, Clarence Road, Norwich. *Single.* He sang a song at the entertainment 11 Sept. Pet name 'Skelly'. Dynamo apparatus. Photographer.

Skelton is a general favourite and in addition to his very arduous engine

17. Reginald Skelton – the Engineer.

room work, he takes charge of the dark room, stores all negatives of interest and, with Wilson, does all the bird skinning.

Party to C. Crozier and Main Western Party. Best of the sledgers, 1903–04. With Captain over inland ice. *Total travelling* – 171 days.

£20.16.8 a month   £250

Views of Dr Koettlitz on scurvy

In Jan 1901 Dr Walter C. Parkes proposed (in the *Guy's Hospital Gazette*) that Guy's men should subscribe £100 to equip a bacteriological laboratory for Dr Koettlitz. By March £19.18.6 had been subscribed.

In the *Guy's Hospital Gazette* for 30 March 1901, Dr Koettlitz, in a letter, supports the theory of Professor Torup of Christiania respecting scurvy: viz that it is a chronic ptomaine poisoning induced by the continuous ingestion of foods which have undergone putrefaction and fermentative changes; that there are no such substances as antiscorbutics, that to prevent scurvy it is necessary to use food free from scorbutic properties, instead of seeking for substances which have ignorantly been called antiscorbutic; that lime juice has not the smallest counteracting effect against attacks of scurvy.

Dr Koettlitz's experience in Franz Josef land bears out the above conclusions in every respect. The crew of the *Windward* all had scurvy and two died. They drank lime juice daily; but fed on tainted meat. Jackson's party had no scurvy and no lime juice, but fed on fresh meat of bears and birds. The experience of Leigh Smith was the same.

In the number for May 1901 Dr G. Newton Pitt maintains a contrary view (the formerly received one) that scurvy arises from a lack of some essential element in food, and not from tainted food. He gives several instances of scurvy disappearing after fresh vegetables were added to the diet. He maintains that it was the use of fresh food, not the absence of tainted food which kept the parties of Leigh Smith and Jackson healthy.

[82]

Reginald Koettlitz
(Sledge Traveller)

(Kent) Born *Dec 23d 1861*, of German extraction. Home at Dover. Born at Ostend. In practice 7 years. An old 'Guy's man'. *Age 40.* 1894–97 Harmsworth Expedition. Surgeon. Appointed 23 March 1900 by me. Botanist & Bacteriologist. Appointed 15 June 1900. *Married.* Riverside, Pencester Road, Dover. He had 2 teeth stopped, and 1 pulled out in July 1901. He sang a song at the entertainment on 13 Aug.

His bacteriological apparatus was presented to him by the former students of Guy's Hospital – £80 subscribed. *Pet name* 'Cutlets'.

Koettlitz is a very honest good fellow, with an exceptional knowledge of his profession and a deal of information on scientific matters, but withal exceedingly short of common sense. On account of his lack of ability to see a joke he gets exceedingly chaffed, but takes it all in good part.

In the sledge reconnaissance party to S.W. *Total travelling 83 days.*

Expedition £400

Edward Wilson
(Sledge Traveller)

(Gloucestershire). Born *July 23d 1872.* Nephew of Genl. Sir Charles Wilson. Surgeon at Cheltenham. Son of Dr P. J. Wilson M.D. (Westal, Cheltenham). Vertebrate zoologist M.B. Report on the birds of Trinidad Id. Artist. *Married* on 16 July 1901 (Suffolk Hall, Westal, Cheltenham) to Oriana Souper. Appointed 19 Dec 1900.

In charge of the Xanthometer constructed by Dr Mill, for measuring the colour of the sea.

[83]

18. Reginald Koettlitz – the Surgeon.

19. Edward Wilson – the Assistant Surgeon.

He had 1 tooth stopped in July 1901.
Wine caterer.

Wilson is a man who will do great things some day. He has quite the keenest intellect on board, and a marvellous capacity for work. You know his artistic talent, but would be surprised at the speed at which he paints, and the indefatigable manner in which he is always at it. He has fallen at once into ship life, helps with any job that may be in hand, doctors the men, keeps one eye to the ventilation of the ship, runs the wine, is great friends with all the young lieutenants, and in fact is an excellent fellow all round.

With Scott in his great S. sledge journey 94 days. *Total travelling 158 days.*

Expedition £200

WAGES

The Expeditionary pay (in addition to their naval pay) of the 32 naval officers and men will be   £2148 a year
Of the 7 other officers and civilian staff £1950 a year
Of the [?] merchant seamen   £ 756 a year

    £4854 for one year
     2

    £9708 for two years
    4854

    £14,562 for three years

OFFICERS

Draft letter of Appointments

Commander Scott and Lieut. Royds received special letters of appointment signed by Lord Lister and myself. The rest received letters of which the following is the draft:

'Sir,
You have been appointed, with the approval of the Councils of the Royal Society and the Royal Geographical Society [*For Naval Officers* "and with the permission of the Lords

Commissioners of the Admiralty". *For Armitage* "and with the permission of the Peninsular and Oriental Steam Navigation Company"] to be [Second in command and navigator *Lt. Armitage*, Executive Officers *Lieuts Barne* and *Shackleton*, Engineer *Mr Skelton*, Drs *Koettlitz* and *Wilson*, Biologist *Mr Hodgson*, Geologist *Mr Ferrar*, Physicist *Mr Bernacchi*.] of the Antarctic Expedition which has been equipped and will be despatched by the two Societies, under the command of Commander Robert F. Scott R.N., F.R.G.S.

Your salary will be [1. 450. 2. 200. 3. 200. 4. 250. 5. 400. 6. 200. 7. 200. 8. 200. 9. 250.] payable from July 1st until the return of the expedition to this country.

[*To the Doctors.* "When not engaged on the duties of your department, you are to assist in the scientific work, under instructions from the Director of the Civilian Staff". *To Civilians.* "You will perform your scientific duties under instructions from the Director of the Civilian Staff."]

You will be required to sign articles in accordance with the provisions of the Merchant Shipping Act, under which the *Discovery* will sail. The articles will contain a clause inserted for the protection of the Royal Geographical Society as owner of the ship.

It is to be understood that all journals, sketches, photographs, and collections kept or made by you are to be considered as the property of the two Societies, and to be delivered to the Commander of the Expedition [*for Civilians* "To the Director of the Civilian Staff"] on demand. You are also to undertake not to publish anything concerning the expedition until six months after the publication of the official narrative.

In volunteering for this arduous service you have, we feel sure, undertaken the duty with the determination of exerting yourself to the utmost, and of using all your abilities and powers for the success of the great objects, for the attainment of which the Expedition is to be despatched.

Be assured that you will find in us steady friends on whom you may rely for appreciation of your exertions, and for assistance in advancing your reasonable wishes and interests.'

	We have &c
Sd.	William Huggins
	(*President of the Royal Society*)
Sd.	Clements R. Markham
	(*President of the Royal Geographical Society*).

The several persons whose names are subscribed agree to serve on board the steam yacht *Discovery* on a voyage to any places in the Antarctic Regions for any period not exceeding five years.

Besides the usual Articles – each and every member of the crew agrees to assist in unloading transferring and taking on board stores and goods, and in erecting and pulling down any structure on shore or on the ice, and will do all work required to further the cause and object of this expedition.

No one to publish any information concerning the expedition within a year from its return. All collections, sketches, journals &c shall belong solely to the President of the R.G.S.

The seamen and firemen shall render mutual assistance in the general duties of the vessel when required.

Each member of the crew takes part in the hazards of this expedition, as regards his person and property entirely at his own risk.

Ship's Company's teeth

The teeth were examined by dental surgeons from Guy's Hospital in July 1901. 178 teeth were stopped, and 92 pulled out. Bill £62.4.5. 41 examinations at the rate of 30s a man.

Ship's Company

'The warrant officers are one and all good men, and the men as fine a crowd as one would wish to see.'

WARRANT OFFICERS

J. H. Dellbridge	(Portsmouth) *Age 29.* Engine Room Artificer. From H.M.S. *Majestic.* He had 9 teeth stopped and 1 pulled out in July 1901.
Letters by *Morning*	Father – John Dellbridge, 97 Powerscourt Road, North End, Portsmouth. Assistant Engineer. *Single.* Will to Father, brothers, and a cousin. *Total travelling 58 days.*

Expedition £5.15.7 a month   £69.7
Navy   £63.17
_____
£133

T. Alfred Feather
(Sledge Traveller)

(Norfolk) born at Great Yarmouth. Age *31*. From H.M.S. *Boscawen*. He had 10 teeth stopped and 6 pulled out in July 1901. Boatswain.

Letters by
Morning

Mother – Mrs Feather, Post Office, Palling on Sea, Stalham, Norwich. *Single*. Will all to his mother.
In the South Depôt party under Barne. A splendid fellow, always cheerful. 1903–04 with the Captain.
Total travelling 105 days.

Expedition £4.8.10 a month   £59.6
Navy   £57.15
_____
£117

Frederick E. Dailey
(Sledge traveller)

(Plymouth) *Age 28* born at Portsmouth. From H.M.S. *Ganges*. He had 4 teeth stopped and 3 pulled out in July 1901. *Carpenter*

Letters by
Morning

Sister – Miss Eva Dailey, 22 Devon Terrace, Bentley, Plymouth
Single. Will. All to his sister. Later address 5 Pole Terrace, Tor Point, Cornwall
In the South Depôt Party under Barne. Promoted to the rank of Carpenter.
Total travelling 72 days

Expedition £4.8.10 a month   £59.6
Navy   £57.15
_____
£117

PETTY OFFICERS

Edgar Evans
(Sledge Traveller)

(Wales) born at Swansea. *Age 26* Came from H.M.S. *Majestic*. He had 3 teeth stopped and 2 pulled out in July 1901.

Parcels by *Morning*	Mother – Mrs S. Evans, 4 Pilton Place, Swansea. *Single. Will.* All to his mother. With Sledge Reconnaissance Party to N.W. Sept 1903
Total travelling 173 days	With Party to Cape Crozier on ski With Main Western Party With Scott's Inland Party 1904

Expedition £3.8.5 monthly	£41.1
Navy	41.3
	£82.4

David Silver Allan	(Scotland) age *30* born at Montrose Came from H.M.S. *Majestic* He had 2 teeth stopped and 2 pulled out in July 1901 He gave a recitation on 11 Sept.
Parcels &c by *Morning*	Wife – Mrs E. B. Allan, 27 Mill Lane, Montrose N.B. *Married. Will.* All to his wife. Feb 1903. Reduced his allotment to £4 per month.

William Smythe *(Sledge Traveller)*	(Hampshire) born at Portsmouth. *Age 27* Came from H.M.S. *St. Vincent.* He had 10 teeth stopped in July 1901 Disrated to A.B.; but re-instated June 1903
Letter by *Morning*	Mother – Mrs E. Smythe, 18, Bath Road, Southsea *Single. Will* all to his mother. In the South Depôt Party with Barne. Very good man. *Total travelling 149 days*

Jacob Cross *(Sledge Traveller)*	(Essex) *age 25* born at Little Clacton. Came from H.M.S. *Jupiter* He had 5 teeth stopped in July 1901
Letters by *Morning*	Mother – Mrs J. Cross, Little Clacton, Colchester (*widow*) *Single.* He sews very well; and gives recitations at the entertainments.

| *Total travelling*
91 days | With the sledge reconnaissance party to W. in Sept
Expert seal and bird skinner.
Rudyard Kipling's coxswain when he wrote the *Fleet in being* |

	Expedition £3.8.5 a month	£41.1
	Navy	£41.1
		£82.2

William
  Macfarlane[20]
Sledge Traveller)

Letters by
Morning

(Scotland) born at Forfar *Age 27*
Came from H.M.S. *Minotaur*
He had 7 teeth stopped and 1 pulled out in July 1901
Father – Mr A. Macfarlane, Police Building, Portich, Glasgow
Single
With the main West Party. Broke down from weak heart. Invalided.

Thomas Kennar
(Sledge Traveller)
Letter by
Morning

(Devonshire) born at Brixham. *Age 26*
Came from *Magnificent*
Mother – Mrs Susan Kennar, 6 Sunberry Terrace, Furzeham Hill, Brixham
Single. Will all to his mother.
In the South Depôt Party under Barne.

NAVAL SEAMEN

Harry J. Baker[21]

(Kent) age 25 born at Sandgate.
Came from the *Vernon*. He had 6 teeth stopped and 1 pulled out in July 1901
Mother – Mrs M. Baker, 4 Garden Cottages, Chapel Street, Sandgate
Single. Will all to his mother. Discharged at *Lyttelton* as objectionable. He ran. messmates did not like him.

	Expedition £2.5.7 a month	£27.7
	Navy	£28.7.11
		£55.14.11

Charles T. Bonner[22]   (Middlesex) Joined from the *Jupiter*. born at Stepney *Age 23*. He had 5 teeth stopped and 4 pulled out in July 1901
He sang a song at the entertainment on 13 Aug.
Brother – Mr Ernest G. Bonner, 54 Lichfield Road, Bow E
Single. Will all to his brothers.
He was engaged to Miss Minnie Greyburne, 43 Moody Street, Bancroft Rd., Mile End
Leaving Lyttelton Bonner fell from aloft and was killed on the spot. The funeral took place at Port Chalmers on Dec 23d 1901

James W. Dell   (Sussex) Born at Worthing, *Age 23*
Came from *Pembroke*. He had three teeth stopped in July 1901. He plays the mandolin. Smart little fellow. Good sewer. Rather too much under the influence of Hubert, an ill conditioned fellow.

Letter by
Morning   Aunt. Mrs E. Bebbington, 35 Church Terrace, North Street, Abergavenny
His chum was Waterman (*whom see*). They correspond.
Single 3 Ashdown Road, Worthing; where his grand parents and aunt live
1904 hurt his arm. In charge of dogs
Young lady Miss Nellie Brown, Railway Terrace, Liverpool Street E.C.

Jesse Handsley
(Sledge Traveller)   (Gloucester) He joined at New Zealand from the Ringarooma.
Brother. Harry Handsley, 34 Magdala Road, Gloucester

*Total travelling
153 days*   In the South Depôt Party under Barne 1904 with Capt

William L. Heald
(Sledge Traveller)   (Lancashire) born at York. *Age 25*
Came from H.M.S. *Jupiter*
Heald learnt ballooning at Aldershot.

	He had 1 tooth stopped and 1 pulled out in July 1901. Sang a song at the entertainment on Aug 13.
Letter from brother Henry by *Morning*	Father – Mr J. Heald, 115 Derby Street, off Waterloo Road, Cheetham, Manchester. His father is Warder at a prison In the Sledge reconnaissance to W. 11 Sept saved Ferrar's life.

<pre>
    Expedition £2.5.7 a month   £27. 7
    Navy   £28. 7.11
                                _____
                                £55.14.11
</pre>

William Peters[23]

age 22 Born at Cork. Came from the *Magnificent*. He had 5 teeth stopped and 7 pulled out in July 1901
A young skulk
Single 2 Panorama Terrace, Cork
brother Samuel – 3 Crosses Green, Great George Street, Cork

George Thomas Vince[24]
Letter by *Morning*

A.B. Joined at the Cape, from the *Beagle*.
Cousin Miss E. Vince, 83 Salisbury Street, Blandford, Dorset
Lost in sledging party, 11 March 1902

Arthur Pilbeam

(Sussex) age 23 Born at Worthing. Came from the *Mars*. He had one tooth pulled out in July 1901. He sang a song at the entertainment on 13 Aug.
Father – Mr William Pilbeam, 29 Cambridge Road, Hastings
Single c/o the Revd Alfred Hodges

John W. Waterman[25]

(Yorkshire) born at Beverley. *Age 21* Came from *Pembroke*. He had 9 teeth stopped, and 5 pulled out in July 1901
Mother – Mrs Isabel Waterman, 3 Kingston Terrace, Norwood, Beverley
Single Dell was his chum *whom see*

Ernest Edward Mills Joyce
(Sledge Traveller)

A.B. Joined at the Cape, from *Gibraltar*. Born 22d Dec 1875 in Felpham Coast Guard Station, Sussex.
Father a coast guard boatman
Mother Mrs F. Joyce, 52 Blackfriars Road, S.E.
Brother Joseph Joyce & a sister.
In the S. Depôt party under Barne.
At the Greenwich naval school 1886–90. In H.M.S. *Sybille* wrecked in Saldenka Bay. In S. African war. *Medal.*

Expedition £2.5.7 a month   £27.7
                                                £28.7.11
                                               ─────────
                                                £55.14.11

Frank Wild
(Sledge Traveller)

Letters by
Morning

Went with Shackles
Swollen head
No more good[26]

Total travelling
125 days

(Bedfordshire) age 28 born at Skelton, Yorkshire. He had two teeth stopped in July 1901. Came from the *Vernon*. He sang a song at the entertainments on Aug 13 & Sept 11. *Anchored* and *Sweethearts & wives*. He wrote a capital letter home, from the Cape. Landed at Trinidad.
Father – Mr Benjamin Wild, Eversholt, Woburn R.S.O. Clerk to the Trustees of the Eversholt Parochial Charity
Single Eldest son. Brother Ernest A.B. 'Monarch' at the Cape. Rupert and Percy boys at home. Sisters Laurie, Annie, and Sis. Lawrence.
In the Sledge Reconnaissance to S.W. In the Party to C. Crozier on *ski*. 23 Oct 1903–04 with Barne

Thomas Soulsby Williamson
(Sledge Traveller)

(Northumberland) Joined from the *Pactolus*. Born *6 Oct 1877. Age 24* born in Sunderland. He had 16 teeth stopped and 2 pulled out in July 1901.
Uncle – Mr Thomas Soulsby, Southey Street, Westoe, S. Shields
Single. 'A well built, tall, strong man, and an excellent working hand. His

character very good up to 1900, when he came a cropper, and lost his badge &c.'

Total travelling
92 days

In the South Depôt Party under Barne
1904 Capt's depôt party

George Beaver
    Croucher

from H.M.S. *Narcissus*
Sister Mrs Evans, 202 Freeman Street, Grimsby.

Letters by
Morning

Allots all to his sister
Single

Thomas Crean
(Sledge Traveller)

Age 25. Joined from the *Ringarooma* at Port Chalmers.
Mother – Mrs K. Crean, Gurticina, Anniscaul, co Kerry

Total travelling
149 days

    Expedition £2.5.7 a month
With the South Depôt Party under Barne

ROYAL MARINES

Gilbert Scott
(Sledge Traveller)

(Wiltshire)
Domestic
R.M.
Mother Mrs Eva Scott, Stapleford, near Salisbury
Single Splendid fellow
In the sledge reconnaissance to W.
In the Main Western Sledge Party 1903–04. In the journey over the ice barrier
Total travelling 99 days
    Expedition £2.5.7 a month

Arthur Harry Blissitt

(Lincolnshire) *Age 23* born at Grantham
Domestic. He had 4 teeth stopped and 2 pulled out in July 1901
R.M. *Lance Corporal*

Letters by
Morning

Mother Mrs Ann Blissitt, Britannia Inn, 37 Robert? Wrawby Street, Brigg
Single

Arthur Quartly
(Sledge traveller)

Born at Baltimore. *Age 28.* Joined from the *Majestic.* He had 3 teeth stopped, and 3 pulled out in July 1901.

Papers & letters
by *Morning*

Sister Mrs S. H. Brown, New Brighton, Staten Island, New York U.S.A.
Single 11 Twyford Avenue, Portsmouth.
Miss Caroline Post, 37 Central Avenue, Tompkinsville, Staten Island, New York, U.S.A.
In the Sledge Reconnaissance to S.W.
In the Party to C. Crozier

*Total travelling
169 days*

In the Main Western Party 1903–04 with Barne

Expedition £3.8.5 monthly	£41.1
Navy	41.1.3
	82.2.0

William Lashly
(Sledge Traveller)

(Portsmouth) *Age 23.* Born at Hambleton, Hants, from *Duke of Wellington*
He learnt balloon work at Aldershott
He had 4 teeth stopped, and 5 pulled out in July 1901. Best man in the engine room.
Wife – Mrs S. Lashly, 18 Dumbarton Street, Buckland, Portsmouth
In the party to Cape Crozier 23 Oct.
With the Captn. Dec 1903
Married
Total travelling 113 days

Frank Plumley

Joined at the Cape, from the *Gibraltar.*
Mother – Mrs C. Plumley, 83 Strood Road, Clevedon, Somerset

Parcels & letters
by *Morning*

1903–04 in Captain's depôt party: then with Royds over the barrier
Total Travelling 106 days.

Thomas Whitfield

(Hampshire) age *32* born at Newport co Salop. Joined from H.M.S. *Resolution.*
He had two teeth stopped and 6 pulled

out in July 1901 19 stone, very big man
Friend. Mr Walter C. Goffe, 66 Glad-
stone Road, Boscombe, Bournemouth
Single

William Page[27]   (Yorkshire) A powerful young fellow of
great muscular development. Sings a
good comic song. Born at Berwick on
Tweed.
Age 25. Joined from the *Royal Adelaide*.
He had 6 teeth stopped and 9 pulled out
in July 1901. He sang a comic song at
the entertainments on 13 Aug. and 11
Sept.
Friend Minnie Buller, 122 Fitzwilliam
Street, Sheffield. Changed to Crown
Inn, Bessemer Road, Attercliffe, She-
ffield
Single Will, all to Miss Buller
Skulk

Expedition £3.8.5 a month	£41.1
Navy	£41.1
	£82.2

William Hubert[28]   (London) *age 35*
Artificer (*not naval*). He had 5 teeth
stopped in July 1901. Teeth scaled.
Wife – Mrs M. E. Hubert, 67 Brabazon
Street, Poplar E (June 1902) 167 St.
Parcels by   Leonard Road, Poplar E
Morning   *Married*
Donkey-man
Pay £7 a month (£84 a year) Allots £5 a
month to his wife

MERCHANT SEAMEN

James Duncan[29]   age *31* born in Perthshire. He had 10
teeth stopped and 5 pulled out in July
1901
Shipwright. Sang a song on Sept 11.
Married. 35 King Street, Dundee.

Mrs May Jane Duncan, 3 young children, a boy and two girls. The wife is a very nice respectable woman, English but her parents live in Dundee. The father has a good post in some leather works. Mrs Duncan will be looked after by Mrs Geo Baxter.
Pay £8 a month. Allots all to his wife.
Expedition £96 a year

Hugh Miller[30]

(Hampshire) born at Rye. *Age 36*
Sailmaker. He had 3 teeth stopped and 3 pulled out in July 1901
Wife – Mrs Elizabeth S. Miller, Yacht Villas, Bath Road, Emsworth, Hants. After Sept 1901 Myrtle House, Bookham, Chichester
Married
Discharged at Lyttelton. Health not quite satisfactory.
Pay £7 a month. Allots all to his wife.
Expedition £84 a year

John Mardon[31]

(Devonshire) born at Brixham. Last served in the *Karamia* of Southampton
Discharged at the Cape
Mother – Mrs Mary Mardon, 6 Furzeham Terrace, Brixham
Single

Robert Sinclair[32]

Joined at the Cape, from the *Oritava* on trial.
Ran because there was something on his mind connected with the death of Bonner.
£5 a month   £60

MEN ENGAGED AT DUNDEE

John Masterton[33]

(Scotland) *age 33* born at Arbroath. Last served in the *Moravia* of Leith
Discharged at the Cape
Wife

	Married – Mrs Mary Masterton, 31 Prince Street, Dundee N.B.
Clarence Hare[34]	Shipped at Lyttelton as Clerk: aged 21. Son of Mr H. Hare of the Bank, Christ Church.
John Walker[35] *(Sledge Traveller)*	(Scotland) age 24 born at Dundee. Came from H.M.S. *Mars* last. He had 8 teeth stopped and 1 pulled out in July 1901 Respectable
Letter by *Morning*	Wife – Mrs Annie Walker, 119 Blackscroft, Dundee N.B. (or 17 Morgan Street?) *Married*. She has gone to live with the mother; being very young. No children. She has given up her own house in Morgan Street. A very nice woman: will be looked after by Mrs G. Baxter Pay £5 a month. Allots all to his wife. In reconnaissance to W.⎫ In Main Western Party ⎭with Armitage Won the medal for *ski* race 'Trustworthy, cheerful, obedient, resourceful'. *Certificate* £60 a year

SCIENTIFIC CIVILIANS

PHYSICIST

Lewis C. Bernacchi	(Tasmania) Born *8 Nov 1876*. Age 25 Two years at Melbourne observatory In the Newnes Expedition Magnetician and Physicist To join at Melbourne with pendulum and magnetic instruments Left England 17 Sept 1901 to join *Cuzco* at Naples F.R.G.S.

Single
Magnetician and Physicist
Arrived at Lyttelton, from Melbourne,
Nov 1901, with all instruments, stores,
dogs &c.
Total travelling, 42 days

£250 a year

BIOLOGIST

Th. Vere Hodgson

Parcel by
Morning

(Birmingham) Born Feby 19th 1864 in
Birmingham. *Age 37*
Curator of Plymouth Museum
April 1901 Cruise in *Michael Sars*
Single 15 Lord's Wood Road, Harborne
Birmingham
Aug 29 he gave a lecture on Maco-
nochie's pickled crustacean.
Pet name *Muggins*
Mother – Mrs J. V. Hodgson, 15
Lordswood Road, Harborne, Birmingham
A bit rough. He possesses a very
thorough and complete knowledge of
his subject, but has much of the
narrowness of a specialist which has to
be rubbed off. He is also quite the most
careless untidy individual it is possible to
imagine; always in trouble about leaving
his things about, or about the really
horrid state of his laboratory. However
when he is sat on he takes it well, and I
think we shall get him all right in time.
Total travelling 19 days

£200 a year

GEOLOGIST

H. T. Ferrar
(Sledge Traveller)

Ireland Born Jan 28th 1879 at Dalkey.
age 22½. Father lives at Pretoria
Cambridge graduate
Geological Student
Physicist Palaeontologist. Geologist –
report on the geology of Trinidad Id.

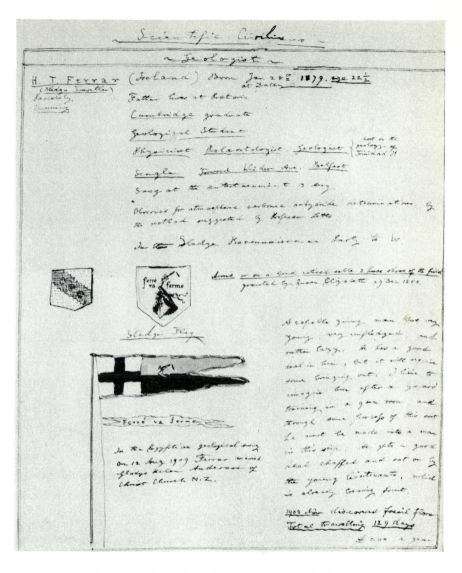

20. An example of how Markham described each of the scientists. This page, for H. T. Ferrar, is illustrated with his coat of arms and his sledge flag (designed by Markham).

Parcels by
Morning

Single Torwood, Windsor Ave, Belfast
Sang at the entertainment 13 Aug
Observes for atmospheric carbonic
anhydride determinations, by the
method suggested by Professor Letts.
In the Sledge Reconnaissance Party to
W.

Sledge Flag
Arms or on a bend
cotised sable 3 horse
shoes of the field
granted by Queen
Elizabeth 29 Dec
1588

A capable young man but very young,
very unfledged, and rather lazy. He has
a good deal in him, but it will require
some bringing out. I like to imagine him
after a year's training in a gun room,
and through some process of this sort
he must be made into a man in this ship.
He gets a good deal chaffed and sat on
by the young lieutenants, which is
already bearing fruit.
1903 Nov discovered fossil flora
In the Egyptian geological survey.
On 12 Aug 1901 Ferrar married Gladys
Helen Anderson of Christ Church N.Z.
Total travelling 129 days

£200 a year

IDLERS

STEWARDS

Edward Else[36]

(Middlesex)
Ship's Steward
In the ship of the Harmsworth Expedi-
tion (*Windward*), also in the *Oceana*
To join at Melbourne with fur clothing
and stores
Wife Mrs Else, 11 Hampton Road,
Forest Gate
Married. His wife being ill, he declined
to go out at the last moment.
Expedition £14 a month   £168

Charles Reginald
Ford

(Middlesex) *age 23* born in London. Son
of a gunner. He had 2 teeth stopped
and 1 pulled out in July 1901

[102]

Navy letters &c	From H.M.S. *Vernon*
by *Morning*	Ward Room Steward & promoted to Chief Steward.
	Accountant
	Sister – Miss Henrietta Ford, 4 Applegarth Road, W. Kensington Park W
	Single. Plays the piano. Type writes. Broke his leg

COOKS

Sydney Roper[37]	(Middlesex) *age 23*
	Ship's Cook He had 9 teeth stopped and 4 pulled out in July 1901. He plays a solo on the mandolin
	Friend – Mrs Noah Crabb, 90 Churston Avenue, Upton Park
	Single Allots £8 a month to Mrs Crabb. At the Cape he changed his mind and now allots to his Mother, Mrs Mary Roper, 25 Ranelagh Road, Leytonstone E
	Discharged at Lyttelton. Objectionable

Henry R. Brett[38]	Ship's Cook, shipped at Lyttelton, age 35.
	Wife & 3 children at Melbourne (231 Grant Street, South Melbourne)
	£6 a month £96

Charles Clark	(Scotland) born at Aberdeen *Age 24* Cook's Mate. He had 6 teeth stopped and 10 pulled out in July 1901
	Laboratory Attendant
	Was Cook at Ben Nevis Observatory
	Professionally he is a baker.
	A good meteorological observer. He volunteered 6 Feb 1901.
	Mother – Mrs Eliz Clark, 53 High Street, Stonehaven
	Father – James Clark, Kincardineshire N.B.
	Single

The Mother wrote too late for her letter to reach *Discovery* at N.Z. She never wrote by the *Morning* though she was twice warned, and then wrote to complain.

£5 a month. Does not wish to allot.

1903–04. With Barne over the barrier

WARD ROOM SERVANTS; AND MAN IN CHARGE OF DOGS

Albert C. Dowsett[39]

Domestic: a good man. *Age 24*
Brother Mr J. E. Dowsett 180 Sutton Court Road, Plaistow E
Single
Discharged at Lyttelton as useless.
£8 a month

Horace E. Buckridge[40]
(Sledge Traveller)

Joined at the Cape, as 'Laboratory Assistant'. *Age 25*.
Brother Fredk. Buckridge, Feron Road, Clapton N. Father and Mother living.
Brother Fredk. a glover & hosier
Went back in Morning 1903
In the South Depôt Sledge party under Barne

Job Clarke[41]

Warrant Officers Mess Servant and to clear laboratories. A useless trash.
Wife Mrs Lily Clarke. c/o Mr Macey, 77 Robsart Street, Brixton S.W.
Married; but wife heart broken because he does not answer her letters. Useless.
£4 a month

F. C. Weller
(Sledge Traveller)

In charge of dogs
Went out to Melbourne in charge of the dogs.
Single. His Father is a pensioner of the Fire Brigade, after a service of 28 years (Orchard Villa, Swanfield Road, Whitstable, Kent)

Letter by *Morning*

He is a sailor. Served 4 years (1895–99) apprenticeship in a vessel trading

between London and the north of England. Since A.B. in steamers on English coast and to Spain. Too short for the Fire Brigade. Fairly good in singing comic songs, and plays the mandolin. Volunteered 4 April 1900.
Pay £5 a month (£60 a year)
Arrived at Lyttelton with the dogs in Nov. 1901.
In the South Depôt Party under Barne
Total travelling 136 days

Letter of Proceedings No. 1.

Discovery
Madeira, Aug 15th

'I have the honour to report that the *Discovery* left Cowes at 11.50 A.M. on Tuesday August 6th, and arrived at this port at 2.30. A.M. today.

Fine weather and favourable breezes have been experienced during the greater part of the voyage, but the swell and sea have been sufficient to indicate that the ship is likely to prove a thoroughly good and comfortable sea boat.

The speed has unfortunately not quite realized expectation. It is doubtful if the ship will average more than 6¾ knots on the passage to Australia, and under such circumstances it becomes evident that the delays at the various ports of call must be made as short as possible, and that less time will be available for deep sea investigations than was hoped for.

Attention had been devoted to preparing the deep sea apparatus for use, and at 5.30 yesterday, the engines were stopped, and the ship hove to under topsails for the purpose of trying the various arrangements. With slight alterations they will, I think, prove highly satisfactory.

Some tow netting has been carried out with satisfactory results.

It is to our great regret that Dr H. R. Mill leaves us at this port. His knowledge and experience have been invaluable in preparing the physical laboratory, and in organizing the meteorological, deep sea temperature and chemical work.

I regret to find my fears confirmed with regard to the defective nature of the various iron fittings of the ship, which were provided by the Dundee Ship-builders Company. The parralls of both lower topsail yards have carried away, exhibiting great carelessness of manufacture.* Arrangements have been made here for their repair, and will, I fear, delay the ship until tomorrow afternoon.

The circumstance is serious, as it is impossible to predict what defects of this sort may not be developed when we arrive in more tempestuous seas.

All on board are in good health and spirits, and it is satisfactory to find that no short comings have as yet been detected with regard to the various stores supposed to be on board.

If time permit I would suggest that another Petterssen water bottle (large type) should be forwarded to Melbourne. Dr Mill could be consulted on the order, and the instrument sent in Mr Bernacchi's charge.'

(signed)
Robert F. Scott
Commander R.N.

*'The goose necks of both our topsail yards have carried away, and are being sent on shore to be welded. The main went first where I have marked a cross. There was a large flaw in it and we had to hang the yard with a sail tackle. The fore did not actually break, but has a crack right round it.'

Michael Barne

'Both the spurs for the lower topsail yards have carried away, and what will go when we get a real breeze of wind it is impossible to conjecture. The faults are owing to gross carelessness in manufacture.'

Scott

Letters from Madeira. SCOTT

Madeira Aug 15th.

My dear Sir Clements,
   We have arrived at Madeira after the most delightful passage. The ship is splendid as a sea boat, quick of movement, but buoyant and most comfortable. Koettlitz is I think the only man who has been sea sick. Though the sea going qualities are excellent, the speed is not quite up to expectation. We only get about 6½ to 7 under steam and sail, whereas I had hoped to

average 7 on the passage out. Our sailing qualities are I fear but poor. The sail area is terribly small so that it would take nearly a gale of wind to produce a respectable speed.

The consequence is that, after a thorough investigation of speed and dates I have come to the conclusion we must hurry the whole way out, and that the time left for oceanographic work won't be much. Murray takes it extraordinarily well. He is perfectly excellent as a messmate and as a director, but *entre nous* is most unpractical in his ideas for working deep sea tackle.

We had a field day yesterday in trying all our gear, and I am glad to say the alterations made in the winches due to the ideas I got, thanks to you, from visiting the *Michael Sars* have proved most efficacious and I believe, with a little practice, we shall be a great deal better at sea work than any ship that has hitherto attempted. We ought to have more Petterssen water bottles and, if funds will allow, I wish you could arrange to send one or even two out to Australia.

I have written a long letter to Smith concerning the enormities of the Dundee ship builders. Both the spurs of the lower topsail yards have carried away, and what will go, when we get a real breeze of wind, it is impossible to conjecture. The articles in question have flaws owing to gross carelessness of manufacture. We are getting repairs done here, and shall be off the moment they are effected – probably tomorrow shortly after noon.

I hoped to get ample time to write letters on the way here but we have been awfully busy getting things straight. I have no doubt you will have a talk with Mill, when you get back from Norway; but it is rather curious that he has been one of the first to suggest the passing over of sea water analysis and temperatures to naval officers. So we have arranged for Shackleton to do the former, and Barne the latter. Royds has a good control of the meteorology, and Mill thinks all will do well in their various tasks. The men are working splendidly and everything is settling into routine with, I think comfort all round.

I hope to write to you a much longer letter from the Cape but you will understand, with the hurry and rush of departure and getting things straight, how limited my time has been. I hope you are enjoying your well earned holiday.

Murray and I have had some discussion about the second ship, and I think his ideas are sound, but I know it will mean much work.

I have so many more letters to get through that I must now

end with my kindest regards to Lady Markham and thanks for her kind letter and message.

believe me
Yours ever sincerely
Robt. F. Scott.

Letters from Madeira. ROYDS

At Sea. 14 Aug 1901

Dear Sir Clements

I meant to have written you a long letter, but we are within calling distance of the island, at least Armitage says so although we haven't sighted him yet, and I shall have only time for a few lines to tell you how we are. We have so far had a regular yachting trip as far as the weather is concerned, and have had sails set since we left the Channel, got into the N.E. trade very early, and have had it light (1–4) behind us ever since. We had a heavy swell in the bay, our maximum roll being 31° to Port, and 24° to Starboard, but no jerk at the finish, just a quiet roll, and everything remained in its place.

We have stopped twice for tow nets; and Mr Murray has been busy with pumping into a net, and there was great excitement over a new 'bird' which they got the other evening. I absolutely get no time for writing, as I am on deck all the forenoon and afternoon with the hands, then I keep the 4 to 8 watch, and then am quite ready to turn in after watch dinner, and am out at four for the morning watch, but am just snatching a few minutes as I must get a letter to you. We had our first sing-song last night, and it went off most successfully, and tonight I believe we are going to try our deep sea sounding and temperature gear.

The belongings for the various departments of science are gradually being unearthed. There is generally a cry out that something has not been sent, and then it is found in the cutter, or some other marvellous stow hole.

I must away on deck again. My love to Lady Markham, and with same to yourself, and you know all I would like to say to thank you for all your great kindness to me and to my people: will write again from the Cape: am very fit, and so are we all.

ever your very affectionately
Charlie Royds*

*He takes things very much to heart and rather worries over

things – does not take his responsibilities lightly – but his enthusiasm and thoroughness are good to see.'

Dr Mill to Miss Royds

Letters from Madeira. BARNE

My dear Sir Clements

The photograph has arrived and is a very good one indeed. It is really very kind of you to give it me. We have had a nice passage with a stiff breeze off the starboard quarter nearly all the way. We have not given her a proper trial under sail alone yet, but hope to before long.

The goose necks of both our lower topsail yards have carried away, and are being sent ashore to be welded.
The main went first where I have marked a cross. There was a large flaw in it, and we had to hand the yard with a sail tackle. The fore did not actually break, but has a crack right round it.

We got in here in the middle watch last night. Yesterday evening we hove to and tried a little sounding. The actual sounding went off very well, but we had a small accident with the brass 'Buchanan' water bottle. We were reeling up by steam with a messenger round the fore windlass and round the driving band of the reel, when a kink came in through the leading block on the davit head, which is a registering block, but when it got to another leading block it stuck and the wire went. There were only 40 fathoms of it through.

We are taking in 60 tons of coal and then off tomorrow night. The engines are a great success, and we have averaged about 7.2 knots under steam and sail.

Please give my kindest regards to Lady Markham. Thanking you for all your kindness

I remain
yours respectfully
Michael Barne

Letters from Madeira. MILL

Madeira 15th. August 1901

Dear Sir Clements

We arrived here early this morning after an extremely pleasant passage, in which the *Discovery* has proved herself to be a remarkably comfortable ship. Even though rolling more than 20°, on one occasion 31°, she has the easiest motion imaginable.

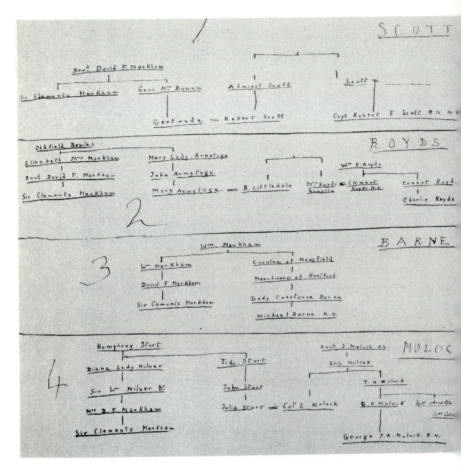

21. Markham was obsessed with genealogy. Here are illustrated his family connections with four of the Expedition officers.

I have got all the physical instruments into working order (i.e. those for observations of the sea) and constructed a proper Xanthometer for measuring the colour of the sea, which Wilson is to use daily. I gave Shackleton full instructions in the salinity work, both with Buchanan's hydrometer and chemically by means of chlorine determinations, and I think he will do the work very well. I made complete tables to supplement those in the Manual, and worked out examples of all the calculations, so that they cannot go wrong.

I have been greatly struck by the ability and enthusiasm of every one on board, and especially by their good nature and mutual good feeling. During the ten days there has not been a jarring note anywhere.

As regards equipment there must be some thermometers for surface temperatures. I cannot understand how Wharton did not supply these, as they are sent to every naval ship and to all merchant ships that keep meteorological logs. A second Pettersons water bottle, to be sent out to Melbourne, would also be of great importance. It is the only exact means of taking deep sea temperatures which can be used, and when there is only one instrument the risk of loss is serious. I shall draw out a list of various minor desiderata, and send it to Longhurst.

Friday August 16

I went out with the little tug which towed the *Discovery* out into the trade this afternoon and cast her off under sail at 6.30. P.M. 4 miles off Funchal. I took photographs of her from several points of view, copies of which I shall send you as soon as they are developed, if they are a success. She set out under rather small sail, the mainsail not being set, and the spanker had to be taken in before she could get before the wind. The people on the tug said she had not sufficient head sail for manoeuvering properly without steam; but as the sailmaker had already remade the jib which did not fit properly, and they have plenty of spare canvas, I have no doubt that want can be supplied easily. As it was she was doing about 3 knots when we left her, and she looked very graceful on the big swell. They gave three very hearty cheers as we let them go; and I certainly felt that every man on board was determined to do all in his power to make the expedition a success.

Yours very sincerely,
Hugh Robert Mill

[111]

4 Collingham Place
South Kensington
8 Sept. 1901

Dear Sir Clements

Thanks very much for your kind letter. I shall strive to do my best to prove worthy of your confidence. With regard to the Petterson water bottle, Dr Mill has very kindly lent the expedition one of his own, which I am taking with me. The observation huts made by the Asbestos Co. were shipped by the P. and O.s *India* and left on Thursday last. Their cost is £100 delivered in Melbourne. I have sent rough plans of them to the Office. The plans and instructions for putting up the huts I have with me. The pendulum apparatus and Eschenhagen instruments will be shipped on the *Cuzco* on Wednesday the 12th, and I am leaving on the 17th to overtake the ship at Marseilles. You will be glad to hear that we have got some splendid records from the Eschenhagen instruments at Kew. They have been running satisfactorily for more than a week. I have also done some work with the pendulums.

I think Sir George Newnes might present his dogs to the expedition if you were to approach him on the subject.

Thanking you again for your kindness, and wishing you good-bye; I remain

Yours sincerely
Louis Bernacchi

Letter of Proceedings No. 2

'Discovery', September 29th. 1901

In continuation of my letter No. 1, despatched at Madeira, I beg to inform you that the *Discovery* sailed from Madeira on Friday August 16th. as soon as possible after the repairs to the topsail yard parralls (which I mentioned as necessary) had been effected. A track chart of her subsequent voyage is attached hereto.

From the 16th. to the 24th. moderately good runs were made under steam and sail, the wind being too light to admit of our proceeding under sail alone.

I had hoped to find the N.E. trade wind sufficiently strong to allow of our saving some coal on this passage and I think that had I decided to pass outside the Cape de Verde Islands we should probably have done so.

From the 24th. to the 30th. we were very unfortunate in experiencing head winds, and as there was no prospect of our making any advance under sail, I began to realize the possibility of grave delay, and the necessity of pushing on with steam at all hazards. This brought a great and unfair strain on the engines and engine room staff. This staff, it is to be remembered, was organized for the actual conditions of service in the far South, where it will not be possible to steam continuously on account of the expenditure of coal. Its number was, therefore, strictly limited to the necessities of intermittent steaming under favourable circumstances.

The temperature in the stoke hold, during the period I have mentioned, was never less than 140°, the engines being new required more than ordinary care and adjustment, and lack of experience of their details further added to the difficulties of an unexpectedly long spell of steaming.

With these conditions the engine room staff worked day and night to avoid a break down, and I have to express my admiration for their efforts, and more especially for the unfailing perseverance and skill of Mr Skelton the Chief Engineer, and Mr Dellbridge the Artificer Engineer.

This anxious time was brought to a close when we crossed the Equator on August 31st., and were able to set sail in the S.E. trade wind.

From that date until September 9th we steered through the trade wind under sail alone, running from 110 to 150 miles daily and gaining some knowledge of the ship's sailing capacity.

It was found unadvisable to keep her close hauled to the wind, on account of the excessive leeway made. She was, therefore, kept about 7 points off, and even thus she sagged away nearly a point to leeward. As a result, and possibly because the trade wind was less favourable than usual, we ran down moderately close to the South American coast. I fear that from this performance the ship must be accounted a poor sailer, and cannot be expected to beat to windward, though she might make a reasonably good passage under sail, with a fair wind.

Since leaving England the ship has leaked considerably. In some part this may be due to faults of construction; but after due consideration, I am inclined to attribute the greater part to the very trying conditions to which she has been subjected. The unequal contraction of the planking due to a tropical sun is evident, especially about the water line. Moreover the intense heat developed in the engine room and stoke hold, in expanding the steel bulk head and girders, cannot but have tended to open the planking in the ship's side.

These conditions were, however, not completely understood in England, and certainly there was a strong impression that the ship would make little or no water; in consequence of which the provisions were stowed close down to the keelson, in the fore and main holds. The water, therefore, which got into the ship, having no space in which to collect, rapidly rose amongst the cases to a height of 2 feet or more.

As soon as this state of affairs was appreciated, I had the holds cleared, and proper floors constructed, with an amply sufficient bilge space beneath.

These steps having luckily been taken in time, the damage to the submerged cases was comparatively slight, and all hands working heartily, the re-stowing of the cases was so satisfactorily done that, despite a considerable reduction of space, the provisions were easily stowed in the original holds. Though the above entailed heavy and trying work on the men and officers in the tropics, I cannot regret its occurrence as it has given us a very exact knowledge of the position of the various stores, and has suggested improvements in the pumping arrangements which are now being carried into effect.

I have placed the stowage of the holds, the general charge of the provisions, and the catering in the hands of Mr Shackleton who is carrying out the work in a most satisfactory manner.

All stores are issued with strict regard to the amounts available for a three year cruise; and under these circumstances it is satisfactory to record that the men are entirely satisfied with their rations, and consider themselves exceedingly well off.

On September 9th steam was again raised and the course altered to the S.E. This course brought the Island of Trinidad ahead, and I decided to touch at it. We sighted the island at day break on Sept 13th, and, standing into the S.W. Bay found a very considerable surf breaking on the shore, but as there was no time available to search for a more convenient spot, I started for the shore with a party of officers and men in two boats at about 10 A.M. and made for a curious rocky promontory described by Mr Knight in his *Cruise of the Falcon*. On this, with some little difficulty, we effected a landing. During our absence the ship was swung by Mr Armitage for the deviation of the compass, and Mr Barne was employed in testing some of the deep sea apparatus.

The landing party were safely re-embarked before dusk. From the 13th to the 18th we made good progress to the southward under steam and sail, in hopes of getting into the westerly winds before the engines were again stopped, but on the 18th our stock of coal being reduced to 35 tons, I thought it best to reserve what remained for possible head winds off the Cape. The wind at this time held in the E.N.E. increasing on the 19th to half a gale until, in a heavy rain squall, it suddenly dropped.

On the 20th it came fairer and we were able to hold our course to the S.E. though not at the speed that could be wished. Since that date we have on the whole experienced fair winds but very shifty, and much lighter than was to have been expected.

The greatest speed yet attained is 9¾ knots, but this was under very favourable circumstances, and as the wind has never held in the same direction or at the same strength for more than 8 or 9 hours, our average speed had been far below this, so that we shall not arrive at the Cape until October 3d.

We have not yet experienced a full gale of wind, but on the 26th it blew very fresh with a heavy sea, and I am pleased to be able to report that the ship proves very stiff and an excellent and most comfortable sea boat.

I mentioned, in my letter from Madeira, that she was not capable of making the speed I at one time hoped for. Taking all things into consideration in the light of a larger experience, I think she has done as well as could be expected from a vessel of her type, and on the whole the wind has certainly been unfavourable to us throughout the passage.

The original date calculated for our arrival at Cape Town was Sept 25th, we shall, therefore, be at least 8 days late.

On the same programme the date of our departure from New Zealand was Dec 4th. If no further delay occurred, the 8 days already lost would postpone that date to Dec 12th. Whereas there is every possibility that further small delays would take place, and it is most desirable that every effort should be made to observe the original date, I have decided to wire for your approval of a step the *pros* and *cons* of which I have carefully considered.

The proposal is that we should make our way direct to Lyttelton, and avoid calling at Melbourne.

The advantages of such a course are that (i) the actual distance of the passage is reduced (ii) The ship will have to be refitted and recaulked whilst a considerable quantity of stores are being received on board. This work can be far more easily and expeditiously performed if a ship is at one place for a fortnight, than if she spent a week at each of two places. (iii) our experience of the delays caused by visitors, and the ill effect of such on the ship's company, is already sufficient to assure me that a visit to Melbourne might in this respect be very inconvenient and trying (iv) Before our arrival in the longitude of Australia I hope to be able to stand to the southward and increase the number of magnetic observations made in the vicinity of what has been supposed to be the focus of maximum intensity. It appears to be a problem of considerable interest, and one which we cannot hope to investigate if we adhere to our plan of calling at Melbourne.

The objections to omitting Melbourne as a port of call are: (i) that it would be desirable to include that place in the chain of magnetic stations that are joined by our observations. There appears no real necessity for this, however, and, as I have mentioned, its inclusion would altogether prevent another important piece of magnetic work being performed. (ii) The second and more important objection lies in the possibility of some failure in the forwarding of the stores now awaiting us at Melbourne.

This would be very deplorable, and I would respectfully urge that every effort should be made to avoid it.

I am forwarding from Cape Town the magnetic, water density, and meteorological observations taken during the voyage, with reports from the officers who have taken them. Any remarks that might be made by experts on these reports would doubtless prove instructive for the future guidance of the observers, and such remarks, if posted without delay, should reach the ship at Lyttelton.

The magnetic observations have been taken more for the purpose of practising with the instruments than with a view to serious work. Mr Armitage has, however, taken every opportunity of preparing himself for the more serious observations to be taken after leaving the Cape, and he will be principally assisted by Lieut Barne.

Lieut Royds has been placed in charge of the meteorological observations, and shows great perseverance in maintaining the routine of observations and in keeping the records in a proper manner.

It will be seen from his remarks that some difficulties are

experienced with some of the less common instruments, such as the ozonometer, dust counter, and evaporimeter.

Lieut Shackleton was instructed by Dr Mill in the use of the hydrometer, and in the chlorine test of sea water. He has been very painstaking in the collection and examination of water samples.

I have placed Lieut Barne in charge of the sounding machines, deep sea thermometers &c, and he will keep the depth and temperature records.

I have to report that the men of the expedition have given great satisfaction with the exception of one merchant seaman J. Mardon. One naval seaman, J. W. Waterman, will have to be invalided.

I have &c
(signed)
Robert F. Scott
Commander R.N.

The Presidents of the R.S.
and R.G.S.

The two Presidents to Captain Scott.

University Building
Burlington Gardens
W
29 October 1901

Dear Captain Scott

We have duly received your letters of proceedings No. 1 dated at Madeira on August 15th, and No. 2 dated at sea on September 29th 1901.

With regard to No 1 serious notice has been taken by the Finance Committee of the unsatisfactory character of the iron work, in treating with the Dundee Ship Builder's Company respecting their bill of extras. In compliance with your suggestion two more Petterson Nansen water bottles have been sent out in Mr Bernacchi's charge.

On the receipt of your telegram from the Cape, announcing your intention to proceed direct to Lyttelton a telegram was sent to Mr Bernacchi at Melbourne, followed by a letter with instructions to forward all stores from Melbourne to Lyttelton, to proceed to Lyttelton himself with the instruments and asbestos huts, and to see that all letters and parcels were forwarded by the Melbourne Post Office.

We have also addressed letters to the Honble C. C. Bowen of Christ Church, New Zealand, a Member of the Legislative

Council, and to the Director of the Magnetic Observatory at Christ Church, requesting them to extend their good offices to the Expedition, and to give you all possible assistance.

We have perused the account of your voyage, in your letter of proceedings No. 2 with great interest. We note the trying conditions in the engine room caused by the unavoidably long spell of steaming in the tropics; as well as the judicious arrangements you have made in the holds, entailing much trying work for the men, in consequence of a leak which, we trust, will be stopped by more careful caulking at the Cape or Lyttelton.

Your expression of admiration for the efforts of the engineering staff; and more especially for the perseverance and skill of Mr Skelton, and of his assistant Mr Dellbridge; and your warm appreciation of the zealous work of officers and men at the time of clearing the holds, as on all other occasions, is most fully shared in by us. We desire that you will convey to all under your command our gratification at the fine qualities they have shown, and our approbation of conduct which gives such high promise for the performance of more difficult and trying duties in the future.

On the whole we consider your report of the vessel, and of her performances under steam and sail to be as good as we had a right to expect. But the much greater consumption of coal than was calculated is a serious matter. We regret that the experience already gained, points to the necessity for increased care in the use of coal after entering the ice. As this appears inevitable you will of course take the expeience you have acquired into consideration, in planning all your future operations.

We have considered the reasons for and against your decision to proceed from the Cape to Lyttelton without touching at Melbourne, and our conclusion is the same as your own. The course upon which you have resolved has our full approval.

We hope to hear that you have had time to stand to the southward on the Australian meridians, and to take magnetic observations near what is supposed to be the focus of maximum intensity, before shaping a course direct to Lyttelton.

The financial arrangements connected with the Expedition, will be the subject of a separate despatch which will be addressed to you by the Finance Committee.

Assisted by Mr Coleridge Farr, your officers will, we trust, succeed in establishing a satisfactory magnetic base at Christ Church. The magnetic observations received from the Cape have been sent to Captain Creak, and the meteorological and water density observations to Dr Mill, for their remarks, which will be forwarded to you by this mail.

You will fill up with coals at Lyttelton, take the dogs and stores on board, and as much live stock as you can possibly carry. We desire to impress upon you the very great importance of supplying fresh food for your people on every possible occasion. We trust that you may be able to leave Lyttelton by the middle of December, and to enter upon the great work of Antarctic Exploration in compliance with your instructions.

Be assured that we deeply feel the great difficulties of the undertaking and the heavy responsibilities of your command. But we have full confidence in your ability, judgment and skill, and that you possess those higher qualities which fit you to lead men in times of hardship and peril, and to secure such a measure of success as the powers of nature arrayed against you may render possible. We ask no more.

We gather from your letters that your officers, and the scientific gentlemen under your command, have already shown that zeal, combined with intelligence which deserves if it does not always command success; and that both officers and men have conducted themselves to your entire satisfaction. Assure them all of our warm sympathy, that they have steadfast friends in us, and that we shall watch over their interests during their absence. You are aware of the efforts that are being made to despatch a relief ship in the season of 1902.

Knowing that nothing will be wanting in your endeavours to secure success, and how nobly you are supported by those under your command, we say farewell with feelings of well founded hope and we shall always remain

Your affection friends
William Huggins (Prest. R.S.)
Clements R. Markham (Prest. R.G.S.)

Commander Robert F. Scott R.N.
Antarctic Ship *Discovery*

Telegram
From Commr. Scott R.N.
Lyttelton 29 Nov 11.40. A.M.
Arrived. All well. From 52°S. and 131°E we went south and entered the pack in 62°S and 141°E. Compelled by time to

return. We called at Macquarie Island. Obtained series of magnetic observations, and some soundings and collections. Ship behaves well in heavy weather and in the ice. Only regret very limited time.

Telegram
    From His Majesty King Edward VII
        to Commander Scott, *Discovery*, 17 Dec 1901
    'The King wishes you all God speed: all success: and a safe return.'

Letter of Proceedings No. 3.

Precis

Off Lyttelton
Nov 28th 1901

On October 14th we left Simon's bay and put to sea amidst the hearty cheering of the whole fleet. On the 21st we were in 45°S in a flat calm and clear bright sunshine. A westerly breeze sprung up in the afternoon, and on the 22d we proceeded under sail alone; passing north of the Crozets. From October 27th to November 3d we experienced a succession of gales from the N.N.W. to N.W. and working round to S.W. At times it blew very hard with heavy cross seas, and the squalls burst in violent storms of wind and hail or snow. As this spell of bad weather may be accounted the first real test of the ship's sea worthy qualities, it is pleasing to record that she proves entirely satisfactory from this important point of view. She rises easily and lightly to the heaviest seas, is wonderfully stiff under canvas, and surprisingly dry. I had expected the possibility of shipping seas over the stern when running before heavy weather, and consequently some risk of broaching to, and am agreeably surprised to find that no such danger exists. The ship in fact proves in all respects a wonderfully good sea boat to the great credit of her designer. For this point might have been easily overlooked in an attempt to follow the lines of modern polar ships, in forgetfulness of the extreme difference of sea conditions in these southern latitudes. I attribute the ease with which she rises to heavy following seas entirely to the rounded shape of the stern, which I think will also give us a great advantage in the ice, notwithstanding the severe criticism it met with in many quarters at home.

A good sea boat is usually what seamen call 'lively' and the *Discovery* proves anything but an exception to the rule. She is tossed about like a cork on the big seas, and we have recorded rolls up to 47°.

During the gales all plain sail was carried on the ship and good progress was made. The greatest run for 24 hours was 223 knots; but 200 knots was exceeded on several occasions.

Such a time has been of excellent service to officers and men in learning to handle the ship and the sails. It has given them confidence in the ship and in themselves which cannot be overvalued. I am glad to think that the charge of inexperience which might so reasonably have attached to the whole crew, in view of the small amount of time they had spent in sailing vessels, can now no longer be applied.

The wind having fallen light we used steam from Novr. 4th to 12th, and gradually increased our southing towards the focus of magnetic intensity. On Nov 12th in Lat 52S. Long 131E, about the centre of this focus, I decided to turn southwards towards the magnetic pole to observe the changes of force. The observations seem to show a very gradual increase of force as the pole is approached, and there are other points of interest in the observations of the dip and variation.

On November 16th the first ice was sighted, the weather dull and thick with driving snow, heavy swell but little sea, ship making 7 knots under plain sail. At 4 a strong ice blink was observed, and in half an hour we ran into a loose pack of drift ice. At 5 sounded and found bottom at 2300 fathoms. At 8 P.M. the pack became thicker and at 9 we were in a close pack, and our way was stopped. Lat 62.50.S – Long 139.40.E. We got up steam and on the 17th we were steaming through streams of loose pack. At 4.30 clear of the ice, and sounded in 2300 fathoms. With the single exception of a small overturned berg, we saw no icebergs, 20th sounded in 1750 fathoms.

We continued N.E. and on the 22d, at 11. A.M. we sighted Macquarie Island exactly at the time and in the direction expected, a satisfactory fact after so long an absence from land. I anchored within half a mile of the shore, and parties landed to make collections. The opportunity was taken of serving out the flesh of penguins for food. Many pronounced it excellent, and all seemed to appreciate the necessity of cultivating a taste for it.

We shall be off Lyttelton tonight (28th Nov). The ship has run over 15000 miles under very varying conditions of temperature, sea, and wind. Today the engines were worked at a considerably greater number of revolutions than they had previously attained even on the official trial. Throughout the voyage we have lost neither a sail nor a rope yarn, nor have we had any accident to the considerable amount of top hamper that is, by necessity secured above the upper deck. For this satisfactory state of affairs I would submit that the greatest credit is due to the officers who have superintended and managed these matters from the beginning, Mr Royds, Mr Skelton, Mr Feather, Mr Daly, and Mr Dellbridge.

Letter of Proceedings No. 4.

At Sea 22d Dec 1902
[*sic*: 1901]

A sad accident has cast some gloom over our final departure from Lyttelton. Shortly after leaving the harbour a young able seaman named Charles Bonner fell from the main truck on to the engine room casing, and was instantly killed. He will be buried on our arrival at Port Chalmers tomorrow.

The magnetic observations were most completely accomplished at Christ Church. They should prove satisfactory, since we had the advantage of taking them under the most favourable circumstances possible.

The Ship's Company were employed, during our stay, in thoroughly refitting the rigging, and stowing the deck cargo, assisted by working parties from the *Ringarooma*. In consequence of Admiral Beaumont's kind wish, and Captain Rich's courtesy every assistance possible was rendered.

On arrival at Lyttelton the *Discovery* was making sufficient water to necessitate more than an hour's work at the hand pumps daily. I could not think it advisable to start on our long voyage with the prospect of such continuous labour. The leaking in the holds and engine room had been continuous since we left England, and a bad leak had been sprung in the fore peak after entering the pack ice. I placed the work in the hands of Mr M. H. Miller who carried it out in the most thorough manner possible, in the limited time at his disposal. On first docking the ship was thoroughly caulked which practically stopped all leakage except in the fore peak.

The results of the examination of the ship are embodied in the Report of Mr Dailey, the Carpenter, and are most discreditable to the ship builders at Dundee.

No improvement having been effected in the fore peak, the

ship was again docked and the bow plates removed. A second Report from Mr Dailey details the work then done. Unfortunately little improvement resulted, and it can only be concluded that some fault exists in the long bolts running longitudinally through the stem. In so far as the leak is concerned, it is now not serious, as the amount of water made can be pumped out in 10 minutes. It is most unlikely to increase and may possibly take up.

The holds are now as full as it would be possible to stow them. We have absolute knowledge of what is on board, and where each particular article is stowed. The ship contains provisions for 2 years and 8 months. By careful stowage we have now in our bunkers 285 tons of coal, besides a deck cargo of 40 tons. A small additional quantity will be shipped at Port Chalmers.

The ship is very heavily laden, but I think not to any extent of risk. Our 23 dogs are safely on board: and also 45 sheep, out of a free gift of 100s offered.

An interest amounting to enthusiasm has been displayed towards the Expedition generally in New Zealand, and the individual and collective hospitality shown to officers and men has been extraordinary. On leaving Lyttelton yesterday we were accompanied by no less than 5 steamers, whilst very large crowds were assembled on the quay.

All on board are anxious to do their utmost in the service of the Expedition, and we shall be supported in all times of difficulty by the knowledge that our interests, and the interests of those who are dear to us will be safe in your keeping. I have &c

(signed)
Robert F. Scott
(Captain)

Letter of Proceedings No. 5.

Port Chalmers 24 Dec 1901

The *Discovery* leaves this port in half an hour's time, having received an additional 25 tons of coal.

Charles Bonner was buried with naval honours, with the assistance of H.M.S. *Ringarooma* at 6. P.M. yesterday December 23d. Captain Rich has very kindly allowed a volunteer to join the *Discovery* in his place. I have further to report the desertion of Robert Sinclair A.B. the reason apparently being owing to his imagining himself in some sort responsible for Bonner's death. He has been very depressed since. I shall take no steps to apprehend him. He is not making any allotment.

I have &c

(signed)

Robert F. Scott

(Captain)

1902 Entered ice in 67°S   Jan 3
      Off Cape Adare   Jan 9
      Wood Bay   Jan 18
      Harbour in 76°30'S.   Jan 20
      Cape Crozier.   Record   Jan 22
      165°W. barrier trended N
      Followed coast to 152°30'W, 76S
      Feb 3 inlet in barrier in 174.W.
      Sledge party to 78.50.   Balloon
      Cape on coast of Victoria land 78.50.S.
      Ship frozen in   March 24
      Sledging began   Sept 2
      Scott's party reached 82.17 in 163.E
      Coast line seen to 83.20
      'Morning' arrived McMurdo Bay Jan 23. 1903.

HISTORY OF THE JOINT COMMITTEE
STRICTLY CONFIDENTIAL

APPENDIX

Rubbish shot here

'What army commanded by a debating Society
Ever escaped discomfiture and disgrace!'

One man, if he is capable at all, is always more capable than a
number of equally capable men working together as a
Committee. He can act more quickly, and his relations with
persons to be employed are simpler.

The dream of professors and pedants that an undertaking is
best managed by a debating society of selected wiseacres has a
never ending fascination, but it is a mere dream.

As soon as the management of an undertaking is handed over
to a talking Committee, the real work must be done by others.
The alternative is wreck and ignominious failure.

APPENDIX

R.S. JOINT COMMITTEE

A

The persistent attack upon Scott

Although the R.S. Joint Committees succeeded in doing no
harm, certainly did no good, and had no effect on the
Expedition in any shape; still they did their worst; and caused an
enormous amount of friction and worry; and their proceedings
cannot be altogether ignored.

At the time that the fatal mistake was made of joining with the
Royal Society, Lord Lister was President, always courteous,
never taking a decided line, and caring nothing. All the mischief
was due to Professor Michael Foster, a plausible and agreeable

man, but an inveterate intriguer. He cared nothing for the expedition, but only thought how most credit could be got out of it for the Royal Society. He was the Senior Secretary. The other Secretary was Professor Rücker, a man of much greater force of character, but with many irons in the fire, unable to give any time to the work, but interested in the magnetic observations. Mr Kempe, the Treasurer, was a perfectly straight honest man, but as a lawyer he considered that he had a brief for the Royal Society, right or wrong; and unfortunately he was entirely guided by mischievous colleagues.

Foster took the lead. His idea was that there should be a large Joint Committee appointed by the two Councils. He said that the powers of the Joint Committee must be defined on very distinct lines, and did not think that frequent reference to the Councils would work. He thought the Committee should prepare a scheme to be submitted as a whole to the two Councils.

I could not see how a large heterogeneous Committee could do executive work, or how an Expedition could ever be organized or equipped on such a plan. As a compromise I proposed a Committee of nine of each Society, 18 in all:

R.S.	R.G.S.
*Lord Lister[12]	*Sir Clements Markham
*Professor Foster	*Major Darwin
*Professor Rücker	*Mr. Hughes
Sir E. Frankland	Sir John Kirk
*Mr. Kempe	*Mr. Cocks
*Sir Joseph Hooker	*Sir A. Hoskins
*Sir John Murray	*Sir L. McClintock
*Sir A. Geikie	*Sir Vesey Hamilton
*Sir R. Strachey	*Admiral Aldrich
*Dr. Sclater	

But Foster insisted upon the larger number; and at last he consented to 12 appointed by each Council. On various pretexts he subsequently added 5 more, the R.G.S. Council adding 4 to keep the balance, so that the R.S. managed to have one more than the R.G.S. The Royal Society 17, the Royal Geographical 16, total 33.

I drew up the Minute appointing the Joint Committee. The general executive business was referred to it, including appointments, preparation of instructions, and disposal of the fund. But I took care to state exactly each subject that was referred to it, so that when all were dealt with the functions of the Joint Committee would cease.

On the Royal Society side the only expert was Sir Joseph Hooker, still with perfect memory and most useful to consult quietly, but no help in Committees owing to his deafness; being aged 82. Sir John Evans has the credit of being a good man of business, but fond of splitting straws. The rest were quite useless to advise on polar matters, on equipment, or on executive work generally. Of the R.G.S. men, Sir Anthony Hoskins, a distinguished naval officer, had great influence at the Admiralty, was judicious and a good adviser. His services proved to be invaluable, so were those of the three Arctic Admirals. I was quite guileless, believing that the Committee would honestly and jointly consider all questions; so at the request of the Hydrographer, I appointed Nares, Aldrich, and Field, little dreaming that they would turn against us and join Wharton's clique; nor could I anticipate that Blanford would also turn against us. Strachey, Parr, and May could never come, so that from the first the R.G.S. Council was in a hopeless minority, but this I did not anticipate. I hoped and even expected that there would be a certain amount of reasonableness, members only speaking or pressing their views on points they understood. I had no idea of divisions or voting, for to settle such details by the votes of such men would be obviously absurd. But I reckoned without the Wharton and Poulton cliques. From the first, however, I saw that some change was necessary. To get executive work done, to fit out an Expedition on such a plan, was obviously an impossibility.

The first meeting of the Joint Committee was on June 26th 1899. It always met in the ground-floor room of the Royal Society. I was in the chair. Sir George Nares announced that his son must be appointed to the expedition; and Sub-Committees were appointed for Geology, Biology, Hygiene, Meteorology, Magnetism, and Oceanography.[43]

The second and third meetings were on October 27th and November 4th [1899], when there were squabbles whether magnetism was the main object, and about the terms of a Resolution which was never passed. Wharton and Murray gave much trouble. Luckily Murray[44] resigned. Nothing done.

It had now become evident, even to Sir Michael Foster, that the unwieldy Joint Committee was quite useless as an executive body. Sir Anthony Hoskins, Sir Michael Foster, and I were appointed to draw up a plan for a small Executive Committee.

All executive work was transferred to this Executive Committee and all initiative as regards appointments and instructions. It was to consist of four persons, two appointed by each Council. If the large Joint Committee had been abolished there would have been some sense in the arrangement, but Foster insisted upon all the proceedings of the Executive Committee being discussed and approved by the Joint Committee. So that it was only an additional complication. However the Executive Committee was appointed by Resolution of both Councils on November 2d 1899. I was to be Chairman with my old messmate Sir Vesey Hamilton as my colleague. The R.S. Council nominated Professor Poulton and Captain Tizard, the Assistant Hydrographer. We met first on November 10th 1899.

R.S. Joint Executive Committee

R.G.S.	R.S.
Sir Clements Markham	Captn. Tizard
Sir Vesey Hamilton	Professor Poulton

Both Committees were quite useless. I called the Executive Committee together on 10 Nov and 1 Dec 1899, and 26 Jan, 2 March, 23 March 1900 to propose appointments and arrange about instalments to the Ship Builders, and other matters of routine. Tizard was in the master line, Master on board the *Challenger*, now Assistant Hydrographer and Examiner of Sub-Lieutenants in pilotage. With a most forbidding countenance he was the villain of the piece. Good at his work and with some ability, he is very narrow minded, and set himself up as an Antarctic authority because he had been among icebergs and seen the edge of the ice, when in the *Challenger*. He was a thick and thin partisan of Sir W. Wharton. One would have thought that a worse appointment could not have been made. But the R.S. officials were equal to the occasion. Poulton was then a close friend of Sir Michael Foster. He had been made a Professor at Oxford, his subject being mimicry of butterflies. He is a dull stupid man, with a genius for blundering, and totally ignorant on every subject that could possibly come before the Committee. He was there, as appeared afterwards, solely to forward the designs of his friend Gregory. It was also divulged, when these people fell out, that Tizard and Poulton had received secret instructions from one of the R.S. Secretaries to do all in their power to increase the authority of the Civilian Director in the Expedition. There was an atmosphere of underhand intrigue.

At the meeting on April 18th 1900 I read the letters from Mr Goschen and the Secretary of the Admiralty consenting to the appointment of Scott and Royds. I then explained their qualifications, and proposed that the Executive Committee should recommend them. Tizard at once became very insolent. He tried to cross examine me about my right to communicate with Mr Goschen, wanted to know my authority for doing so, and then broke out against Scott, declaring that he could not sail a ship, that he could not navigate, that he could not survey, and that he was quite unfit. In point of fact the traducer knew nothing about Scott's qualifications. This was rather more than I could stand. In the evening I wrote Tizard a letter, giving him a piece of my mind.

The Joint Committee met on 4th Dec and 15 Dec 1899, and Feb 14th 1900, without doing any particular mischief. At the next meeting on May 4th I moved the appointment of Scott as Commander of the Expedition and Royds as First Executive. Then a regular row began. Tizard had gone complaining to the Royal Society officials with my letter, and excited their jealousy about my writing to Mr Goschen without consulting them. Directly I sat down Professor Rücker got up and delivered a carefully prepared attack upon me. He began by praising my exertions. He said he wished to acknowledge them fully, but at the same time he must complain of my exacting conduct. First I was not satisfied with the members of the Committee. So they were reduced to please me. Then I was not satisfied with the transaction of business, so the Executive Committee was created to please me. But nothing would satisfy me. Now I wanted to have control of correspondence with the Government. He declared he would write and tell the Treasury and Admiralty that no letters were genuine unless signed by both Presidents. Finally he read out the letter I had written to Tizard letting him know what I thought of his conduct in attacking Scott, and complained of my treatment of that inoffensive creature.

I did not condescend to reply to all this insolence, beyond suggesting that the proposed letter to the public offices might be mischievous. But the wrangling went on, Wharton, Tizard and Nares attacking Scott's appointment and others joining. At last Sir John Evans, the R.S. man of business and common sense, proposed that the question should be settled by a Committee of the Naval Officers who were members of the Joint Committee. This was agreed to.

A more futile or unpractical suggestion could not have been

made. There were six distinguished Naval Officers, most of them with Arctic experience, who would insist upon Scott's appointment. Wharton's Hydrographic Clique also numbered six, and they would strive to secure a job for the survey department with obstinate perversity. There could be no sweet reasonableness here. Nothing but the abstention of some of the less valid members of the Clique could settle it.

The Naval Committee met, with Sir L. McClintock in the chair, but Wharton and Tizard were obstinate. They put forward names of officers in their Department, four – one after the other, who were unfit, had not volunteered, and had not been asked if they would volunteer. McClintock said there was no use in continuing the meetings. I saw the R.S. Secretaries and told them that if Wharton was allowed to continue the dead lock they would be responsible. But they could do nothing with him. At last I persuaded McClintock to have one more meeting and divide. The Committee met once more on May 24th, when both Wharton and Tizard heard some home truths. Some of the Clique were ashamed and staid away (Field and Aldrich). Captain Creak has always been luke warm. On a division there was a good majority for Scott's appointment, Wharton and Tizard being the only dissentients.

I called a meeting of the Joint Committee on May 25th 1900, when Scott, proposed by me and seconded by Lord Lister, was unanimously recommended to be Commander of the Expedition, and was appointed in a letter signed by the two Presidents.

NAVAL OFFICERS COMMITTEE

Regular line
1. Admiral Sir Anthony Hoskins (ex First Sea Lord)
2. Admiral Sir Vesey Hamilton (ex First Sea Lord and Arctic)
3. Admiral Sir Leopold McClintock (Greatest Arctic authority)
4. Vice Admiral Markham (Arctic)
5. Captain May R.N. (Arctic)
6. Captain Parr R.N. (Arctic)

Hydrographic Clique
1. Rear Adml. Sir W. Wharton (Hydrographer)
2. Captain Tizard (Asst. Hydrographer). (Wharton's jackal).
3. Captain Creak (*Neutral*). (Magnetician)
4. Captain Field (Surveyor). (Under Wharton's thumb)
5. Admiral Sir George Nares (In the *Challenger*. Arctic)
6. Rear Admiral Aldrich (In the *Challenger*. Arctic)

On the 16th of May [1900] I had a meeting of the Executive Committee and again on the 3d and 8th of June, and on the 15th of June I called a Joint Committee for the appointment of Royds and Skelton. To my great surprise I was harassed about the appointment of Royds in a quarter from which I least expected it. They did not know about him, he was too young, and there was no hurry. Even my old friend McClintock was persistent and obstinate about it. Curiously it was Professor Rücker, no longer on the war path, who came to the rescue!! Really it was important that there should be no more delay about these appointments.

When Scott got to work it was necessary to get rid of the Committees altogether as regards executive work, financial business, and appointments. On November 14th 1900 I got the Executive Committee to adopt Scott's scheme; and on the 20th it was passed by the Joint Committee, though not without much worry and friction. Wharton began by wasting an hour and a half on verbal alterations intended to annoy Scott, in a document which no one would ever see again. Then Nares called for a plan of operations before he would consent to anything. Then up rose another wearisome bore. This was Mr Buchanan, who was physicist on board the *Challenger*, a man of considerable ability in his own narrow line, but unpractical, ill-tempered and self opinionated. His features are exactly like those of a bird of prey. In a loud provoking voice he moved that the proposal of Scott should not be passed until the plan of operations had been considered. This would have stopped all work. As nobody seconded his motion he flounced out of the room. The Committee raised no objection to the arrangements proposed by Scott, thus acknowledging their own incapacity to do the work referred to them by the Councils.

These approvals of the Joint Committee were merely formalities. Scott's scheme was made law by Resolutions of the two Councils on November 26th 1900.

On the 7th of December I strongly urged the R.S. Secretaries to agree to the abolition of the mischievous Joint Committee, but they replied that they must first have that Committee's proposal for the Instructions. In that refusal was contained much power for future mischief and annoyance: and another five months of worry and trouble.

Subjects originally referred to the Joint Committee, May 1899 –

All disposed of.

1. Scope of the expedition. Time of starting. Length of time to be occupied. Work to be done.

Transferred to Select Committee 26 April 1901. *Dealt with.*

2. Organization. Number to be employed. Number in each department.

Transferred to the Commander Nov. 26. 1900. *Dealt with.*

3. Ship to be employed. Fittings. Boats.

Ship Committee. The Joint Committee never meddled. Met first 10 April 1899. *Dealt with.*

4. Stores, provisions, & clothing required.

5. Executive officers and Ship's Company.

6. Scientific Staff

Transferred to Commander Nov 26. 1900. *Dealt with.*

7. Instruments. Deep sea sounding and dredging apparatus.

Transferred to Commander Nov 26 1900. *Dealt with.*

8. Sanitary including warming apparatus.

Transferred to Commander Nov 26. 1900. *Dealt with.*

9. Preparation of scientific instructions to observers

Manual edited by G. Murray under superintendence of Sir Clements Markham Nov 21. 1900. *Dealt with.*

10. Landing party

Transferred to Select Committee April 26. 1901. *Dealt with.*

11. Disposal of Antarctic fund.

Transferred to Joint Finance Committee, Nov. 26 1900. *Dealt with.*

APPENDIX

B

The attempt to wreck the Expedition

The Expedition was exposed to the greatest danger from a determined and carefully planned intrigue for placing a geologist named Gregory in virtual command. The chief conspirators were Sir Michael Foster from love of intrigue, Geikie, Poulton, Wharton, Tizard, and Buchanan.

Gregory was Head of the Geological Department at the British Museum. On October 12th 1899 he wrote to me requesting I would write a testimonial for him, with regard to his fitness for the post of Professor of Geology at the Melbourne University, and send it, with a letter, to the Agent General of Victoria. I was told that my letter was helpful in obtaining him the appointment.

I was able to say that Gregory had shown great perseverance in conducting an expedition to the rift valley and Mount Kenia, and had done very valuable work in physical geography; that he accompanied Conway's expedition to Spitzbergen, again making important physical observations, this time on ice action; and that he had read some interesting papers on two or three occasions at R.G.S. Meetings. I believed him to be an excellent geologist and physicist.

It then occurred to me that Dr Gregory D.Sc. might do for the post of Director of the Civilian Staff, a post which I intended to be identical with that of Sir Wyville Thompson on board the *Challenger*. On November 24th 1899 I saw Gregory at 1 Savile Row, and suggested the appointment to him. He is a little man with a very low voice, always nervously pulling his moustache, and does not inspire confidence; but his scientific ability is undoubted. Yet I felt doubtful. He was just going to Australia, having obtained the Professorship. From Port Said he wrote a long letter to Professor Poulton dated January 19th 1900, to be shown to me. It stated his view of his position as Director, with reference to the other civilians, quite correctly; and on March 16th I wrote to tell him that his letter was approved (of course as regards his own position) and that it was intended that he should be Director of the Civilian Scientific Staff. The rest of Gregory's letter goes over all the work of the Expedition with opinions on the routes, the choice of a captain, the command of a landing party, and many other matters touching which he could know nothing, and which did not concern him. It was the letter of a very self sufficient person, and made me more doubtful. Gregory has since alleged that it contained conditions and stipulations. This is not the case. It merely contained suggestions. On February 14th 1900 there was a meeting of the Joint Committee, at which the appointment of Dr Gregory to be Head of the Civilian Staff was approved. Several letters passed between Gregory and myself respecting the other Members of the Civilian Staff, and it was settled that Gregory should come home for six weeks to organize the scientific work within his department. He arrived from Melbourne on December 5th 1900.

The profligate intrigue then commenced very quietly at first. On December 11th, and again on the 18th I had long conversations with Gregory. He talked much about a landing party, but did not show his hand. Meanwhile he never did a single stroke of the work for which he had come to England, namely the organization of his department, nor did he touch it during the whole time he was here. He was busy with his intrigue, conspiring with Poulton and others. I now found that he was a man of a very nervous temperament, that he still suffered from the effects of tropical fevers, that he had neither experience nor qualifications for the command of men, that he had no head for organization, and that a serious mistake had been made in selecting him.

The attack began with an exchange of views between Gregory and Scott. Then Gregory wrote to me that he was unable to concur in the view taken by Scott, and asked my advice. My reply was that he had better state his own view clearly and explicitly. For a long time I could not get any clear statement out of him. He beat round the bush, saying that Sir Wyville Thompson's instructions were not sufficient, that the circumstances were different. At last he sent me the draft of what he thought the Instructions should be, on January 22d 1901. It was quite inadmissible. He wanted a position equal to Scott, to have a deciding voice as to the route, to be consulted in everything, to have charge of observations and sole command on land, but he conceded that Scott might be in charge during times of stress and danger at sea. The first duplicate collection was to be given to Melbourne University, and Gregory was to be free to communicate discoveries to any newspaper or magazines he chose. I sent the draft back, telling him it was out of the question.

Poulton then began to write letters, and the intrigue developed. They wanted to drive Scott into resignation. They actually wrote to Armitage asking, if Scott resigned, whether he would be captain of the ship, with Gregory commanding the expedition. Armitage replied that he had received the Murchison award for loyalty, and that he had no intention of forfeiting that character.

When their preparations were in progress, Poulton wrote to me, asking that there might be no delay in bringing the Plan of Operations and the Instructions before the Joint Committee. I thought this reasonable.

I had written my Plan of Operations in 1897. As Wharton, Nares, and Buchanan said they were so anxious to consider the point, I asked them to write their own plans, which they did. Wharton merely wanted the ship to cruise along the edge of the ice from the Greenwich meridian westward and winter at Buenos Ayres. He maintained that she ought not to go near Victoria Land, and put forward arguments against a landing party. These two latter opinions should be remembered, with reference to his subsequent conduct. Sir G. Nares was in favour of trying to push the ship southwards to Weddell's furthest. The bird of prey would put a party on shore, he did not say where, then take the ship out of the ice, fill her with wire and dredge for the rest of the time. So much for the views of these precious experts. Nares's plan is the only one which could even be discussed. I bound them all up as a pamphlet with a map, summoned the Executive Committee to meet on December 19th 1900, and my Plan of Operations was unanimously adopted.

On January 30th 1901 I again summoned the Executive Committee to meet and consider the Instructions I had prepared in 1897, with some slight alterations. It was the last time this Committee met. My Instructions were adopted by the three Members present. Poulton was absent. Gregory was there and announced his dissent, but I could not get him to state clearly to what he objected.

I resolved that, under no circumstances, should Dr Gregory be a member of the Antarctic Expedition.

I sent copies of my Plan of Operations and Instructions, both adopted by the Executive Committee, to the Members of the Joint Committee on January 31st 1901.

The plot now began to thicken. But the proceedings were carefully kept secret from myself and the loyal R.G.S. Members of the Joint Committee. The Conspirators worked and intrigued in secret, making up their majority, and formulating their scheme. Sir Michael Foster was in his element, for an intrigue calculated to secure more credit for the Royal Society was approaching maturity, and Poulton had hitherto been his willing agent in similar plots.

The great mistake made by the conspirators was to assume that the Joint Committee was an independent body; whereas the two Councils, which appointed it, could and would reverse any mischievous work it might attempt to do. They also trusted to Sir Michael Foster who turned upon them, and proved a broken reed. However they went confidently forward on their foolish course; trying to burn *our* house down, to roast *their* egg.

Gregory and Poulton were very busy, making mis-statements about the letter of January 19th and about me, writing letters and interviewing. The Hydrographic Clique was ready to do anything against Scott, the Royal Society officials would support measures which appeared to give more importance to what they called science, the three geologists would accept Gregory's stories and support him, and the rest would follow the R.S. officials. They could rely upon a large majority; as there were four deserters from the R.G.S. Council.

Gregory demanded to have equal authority with the Commander as regards the operations and the routes, to have sole command on shore, with some other conditions, and, if they were not conceded he would resign. Having dictated his terms, the R.S. officials called together a secret Caucus consisting of the R.S. members of the Joint Committee, and the two R.G.S. members who were known to be deserters, Nares and Blanford. It was resolved to concede all Gregory's demands, and a Sub-Committee of Wharton and Geikie was appointed to make the necessary alterations in my Instructions. These alterations were printed, and Geikie was told off to move them and force them through. The effect would have been to wreck the expedition and make it a mere trip for their protegé Gregory. The secret was well kept. The R.G.S. members, except the known deserters, were in complete ignorance, and the whole plot was to be sprung upon us and forced through. Longhurst, whose duty it was to attend all meetings, was not summoned.

The Joint Committee met on February 8th 1901. Lord Lister had been succeeded by Sir William Huggins who also was courteous, indifferent, and ready to let things drift. One was figure head during the attack on Scott, the other during the more discreditable Gregory job. Professor Rücker and Sir John Evans were abroad. So was Sir L. McClintock on our side.

Be it remembered that none of the ringleaders, Foster, Wharton[45] Geikie, Poulton, Tizard or Buchanan had subscribed a farthing to the expedition.

On the 8th Geikie proposed the alterations in my Instructions. The R.G.S. Members asked for time to consider the radical revolution that was thus violently sprung upon them. This reasonable request was opposed; and Geikie said he would pass his resolutions if he sat there until midnight. But the R.S. officials were rather ashamed of themselves, and the meeting was adjourned for four days.

The Joint Committee met again on February 12th 1901. Sir Archibald Geikie again moved his alterations, supported by Sir W. Wharton the Hydrographer. There were a number of verbal alterations – all mischievous, all intended to lower Scott's position. But the main point was the cutting out of all my paragraphs explaining the work to be done during the navigable season, and leaving the procedure of the expedition, especially as regards wintering, to the discretion of the Commander. In their place were to be substituted orders for the ship to waste all the navigable season in landing Gregory in command of a shore party, for the ship then to return direct to Melbourne, and to go back for Gregory in the following year!! It was an attempt to wreck the expedition in order to gratify Gregory's ambition.

Geikie was the proposer. Wharton, the seconder had only a few weeks before written and printed views diametrically opposed to having any such landing party. There was no pretence of either consistency or decency among these jobbers.

Sir Michael Foster then proposed that the Plans of Operations should not be considered apart, but with the Instructions. In point of fact they were not considered at all, and mine was tacitly adopted.

None of the necessary details had even been considered. Geikie and the other ringleaders were shamefully ignorant of what they were proposing. Sir Vesey Hamilton asked how long it was calculated that it would take to land three years provisions and coals on the coast of Victoria Land. Geikie pretended not to hear. When the question was repeated he answered 'Ask one of your Admirals.' He was also rude and discourteous to me.

Poulton got up and began to read a private letter from me. I protested against this being done without my consent.[46] He persisted and I then said that I should be obliged to leave the meeting. *'Then go'!* shouted Geikie in a rude tone of voice. The next exhibition was made by the bird of prey, who was perched at the end of the table. He got up and informed the Committee that my word was not worthy of consideration. I thought this was about enough, so I left the room, with no intention of again taking part in the squabbles of this precious Joint Committee. The real battle would have to be fought out elsewhere. I did not care what such people did or said, and would have remained if my presence could have been of the slightest use. But it could not. The conspirators had organized their majority, and were going to vote us down.

After I departed the R.G.S. Arctic Officers moved that, before this Gregory landing party was decided upon, the effect it would have on the other exploring work during the navigable season should be considered. They were voted down. The rest of the proceedings were of the same character. Finally all the alterations proposed by Geikie and Wharton were passed by a large majority. His High Mightiness was awaiting the decision upstairs. A ridiculous farce was then enacted. The Committee deputed Professor Poulton and Sir A. Geikie to wait upon the great man, to inform him that all his demands had been complied with, and to express a hope that he would not resign. Professor Gregory condescended to accept on his own conditions. He went out to Australia again, in a fool's paradise, thinking he had gained a complete victory.

Honourable men were thoroughly disgusted with the proceedings and jobbing of this Joint Committee, and refused to have any further connection with it. Admiral Sir Anthony Hoskin wrote to the R.S. President as follows:- 'As the proceedings of the Joint Committee have lately taken a form which I cannot but regret, and with which I feel that I cannot be any longer associated, I beg to withdraw my name as a Member.'

Admiral Sir Vesey Hamilton and Admiral Markham, two distinguished Arctic Authorities, also withdrew their names and gave their reasons in more detail.

I also gave my reasons to the R.G.S. Council for my decision not again to attend the Joint Committee; which were not personal. Considering the gross irregularity of their proceedings, the way in which they made all the interests of the expedition subservient to the demands of their protegé, and their incapacity, I felt that a seat in such a Committee was no fit place for the R.G.S. President, nor for any one who had the interests of the Antarctic Expedition at heart.

Majority of the Joint Committee for the Conspirators

MAJORITY
Royal Society
  Official
1. Sir William Huggins *R.S. Prest.*
2. Sir Michael Foster *R.S. Sec.*
   Professor Rücker *R.S. Sec. absent abroad*
3. Mr. Kempe *R.S. Treasr.*
4. Sir Joseph Hooker *R.S. ex Prest.*
   Sir John Evans *R.S. ex Treasr. absent abroad*
   Ringleaders
5. Sir Archibald Geikie
6. Sir William Wharton
7. Professor Poulton
8. Mr Buchanan
9. Mr Teall
10. Captain Tizard
11. Sir George Nares *R.G.S. Deserter*
    Sheep
12. Captain Creak
13. Admiral Aldrich ⎫ *R.G.S. Deserters*
14. Captain Field ⎭
15. Mr Buchan.
16. Mr Blanford *R.G.S. Deserter*
17. Professor Herdman
18. Dr P. L. Sclater
19. Mr Scott

MINORITY
Royal Geographical Society
  Official
1. Sir Clements Markham *R.G.S. Prest.*
2. Major Darwin *R.G.S. Sec.*
3. Mr. Hughes *R.G.S. Sec.*
4. Mr Cocks *R.G.S. Treasr.*
   Naval and Arctic Authorities
5. Sir Anthony Hoskins
6. Sir Vesey Hamilton

7. Admiral Markham
8. Mr Howard Saunders
9. Sir Leopold McClintock *absent abroad*
10. Sir R. Strachey ⎫
11. Captain May   ⎬ *unable to attend*
12. Captain Parr   ⎭
13. ⎫
14. ⎬ *Four deserters*
15. ⎪
16. ⎭

R.S. available   – 19
R.G.S. available – 8
                  ─────
R.S. majority   11

On February 17th [1901] I again wrote a confidential Memorandum to the Royal Society urging them to consent to the abolition of the mischievous Joint Committee.

As soon as Gregory had started for Melbourne on February 14th, the conspirators began to think they had gone too far. They certainly had gone considerable lengths. The Joint Committee had meetings on February 19th and 26th 1901. Major Darwin, the esteemed R.G.S. Secretary, seemed to have an idolatrous veneration for the Royal Society. So he was anxious to smooth matters over. He moved Resolutions to soften down the proposed new clauses in the Instructions. 'Though the Commander was to bear in mind the importance of Gregory's landing party; yet if the difficulty of landing was very great, he was not to lose sight of the fact that geographical exploration was another primary object of the expedition', also 'if an examination convinces you that a party could not be landed, you are to turn your attention to exploration'. To the paragraph prohibiting the ship to winter was added 'if it can be avoided.' These weakening provisos made the previous alterations futile.

Poulton, Buchanan, and Tizard were sharp enough to see this and were furious. The new provisos upset the whole plot. The Commander could now practically do as he pleased. But Sir Michael Foster proved a broken reed. Geikie and Wharton, after all their bluster, also crawled down. Major Darwin's amendments were carried, while Poulton and his friends entered a protest on the Minutes.

The altered Instructions, with the weakening provisos, were

then sent to the Councils of the two Societies as the final recommendation of the Joint Committee.

Sir Michael Foster next proceeded to address to the R.G.S. Secretaries about the most audacious letter on record, dated March 25th 1901.

'The R.S. President and Council', he informed us, 'are led to understand that great difficulties have been met with on account of the conflicting views which obtain among the members of the Committee, in respect both to the relative importance of the several objects to be gained by the Expedition and to the best way of securing these objects.' He then informed us of the high and noble motives of the R.S. President & Council, and then proceeded 'They have complete confidence that the Joint Committee has carried on its labours in the same spirit, and that its decisions, even if they do not seem wholly to satisfy the wishes of those devoted to this or that branch of knowledge, are the best decisions that can be come to under the circumstances. They are, therefore prepared to give their cordial approval to the Instructions.'

The R.G.S. Council was not prepared to do anything of the kind. I should have positively refused to sign them. The Instructions of the Joint Committee represented the schemes of jobbers watered down by subsequent vacillation and compromise, and were in abominably bad English.

I wrote a Memoir on the subject for the information of the R.G.S. Council, and two long letters of remonstrance to Sir William Huggins, one giving him a detailed history of the events connected with the expedition since 1897; and the other explaining the reasons which made it impossible to give Gregory the command of a landing party.

On March 27th 1901 the R.G.S. Council proposed a Resolution requesting me to inform the Royal Society that serious objections had been raised to the recommendations of the Joint Committee, and to propose a conference between myself, with two Members of the R.G.S. Council, and the R.S. President with two Members of the R.S. Council. The Royal Society consented to this conference. But I wanted a man to manage them all.

'Want you a man!
Experienced in the world and its affairs.
Here he is for your purpose.'
Old play

[141]

APPENDIX

C

How the Pilot weathered the Storm

By this time I was quite exhausted by the friction and worries caused by the Joint Committee. Added to the real work connected with the Expedition it was too much for me. I looked anxiously round for help. The ablest man on our Council was Sir George Goldie. If he would but take the matter in hand we should be safe. Cool and collected, seeing his adversary's moves as clearly as his own, great as a diplomatist as well as an administrator, quickly taking the measure of all with whom he has to deal, absolutely impartial, mastering his brief rapidly and never losing a thread, he would turn the R.S. officials round his finger with perfect ease.

At first he was disinclined to take it up. He did not take much interest in the Antarctic Regions. But he kindly yielded to my solicitations. When he had once consented, he became as keen as a hound, and mastered the whole subject in all its bearings in no time. He would soon take us off the lee shore.

On April 10th 1901 the Conference met at the Royal Society rooms. I had nominated Sir George Goldie and Sir Leopold McClintock. Sir William Huggins had nominated Sir Michael Foster and Mr Kempe.

Conference

Royal Geographical Society	Royal Society
Sir Clements Markham	Sir William Huggins
Sir George Goldie	Sir Michael Foster
Sir Leopold McClintock	Mr Kempe

I began by explaining the points on which we must insist. McClintock added some weighty remarks on the importance of the ship wintering. They then turned to Goldie and asked him to state his views. He civilly declined until he had heard what they had to say. They had little to say, and he then began to twist the professorial tails very courteously but with marked effect. They had to learn the absurdity of wanting to have two Heads to one expedition. He touched lightly on their Secret Caucus. They winced but declared that they went from it to the Committee with open minds. Goldie informed them that that was contrary to all experience of human nature. When they had been sufficiently prepared, he made his proposal. The R.G.S. President, representing the Council and the great mass of the subscribers, should write to the Joint Committee, informing them that their version of the Instructions was inadmissible, and asking them to request the two Councils to appoint a Special Committee of six, to prepare Instructions which should be final.

To my surprise the Royal Society Officials promised to be neutral. The intrigue had failed, and Foster was ready to desert his Poulton. He was probably sick of the whole business. But he would have to eat his leek. Pilot Goldie intended that they should be a good deal more than neutral.

Sir George Goldie drafted the letter to the Joint Committee. It was adopted by the R.G.S. Council on the 17th of April and signed by me. Although our Pilot intended to make the Joint Committee eat its own words with unanimity though with wry faces, it was thought as well to fill up vacancies. The three Admirals who resigned, together with Sir Richard Strachey and Captains May and Parr who resigned at my request owing to inability to attend, made six vacancies. I filled them up for the occasion. I might have added another as the Royal Society had one more than they had a right to. But this would give a majority, added to the Royal Society Officials. We ought to have told our four deserters (Nares, Aldrich, Field and Blanford) that their services were no longer required, and filled up four more vacancies, but it was as well to avoid this if it was not absolutely necessary. Now that the trouble was over, the desire was to do all that was possible to promote peace and conciliation.

The Joint Committee at its last gasp

Party of Pilot Goldie
1. Sir George Goldie *(the Pilot)*
   R.S. Officials
2. Sir William Huggins *(Prest. R.S.)*
3. Sir Michael Foster *(Sec R.S.)*
4. Professor Rücker *(Sec R.S.)*
5. Mr Kempe *(Treasr R.S.)*
6. Sir Joseph Hooker *(Ex Prest R.S.)*
7. Sir John Evans *(Ex Treasr R.S.)*
   R.G.S. Officials
8. Major Darwin *(Sec R.G.S.)*
9. Mr Hughes *(Sec R.G.S.)*
10. Mr Cocks *(Treasr. R.G.S.)*

Voters

11. Sir Leopold McClintock
12. Mr Howard Saunders
13. Sir George Robertson
14. Mr Sutherland Mackenzie
15. Colonel Church
16. Mr Warington Smyth
17. Dr Keltie

Party of Wrecker Poulton

1. Professor Poulton *(Chief Conspirator)*
   Ringleaders
2. Sir Archibald Geikie ⎫ *backing out*
3. Sir William Wharton ⎭
4. Sir George Nares – *backing out, R.G.S. deserter*
5. Captain Tizard ⎫ *out & out jobbers*
6. Mr Buchanan ⎭
7. Mr Teall – *backing out*
   Sheep
8. Mr Buchan ⎫
9. Professor Herdman ⎪
10. Dr. P. L. Sclater ⎬ *Followed R.S. Officials*
11. Captain Creak ⎪
12. Mr Scott ⎭
13. Admiral Aldrich ⎫
14. Captain Foot ⎬ *R.G.S. deserters now adrift*
15. Mr Blanford ⎭

The Joint Committee met on April 26th 1901. Sir George Goldie, after the R.G.S. letter had been read, proposed that the Councils should be requested to appoint a Committee of six to prepare the Instructions, and that its decisions be final. In other words the Joint Committee was voluntarily to reverse all it had done, and acknowledge its incapacity to draw up proper Instructions. Our Pilot made a very able and conciliatory speech, though perhaps a little sarcastic. Then came the fun. The R.S. Officials had only agreed to be neutral. Only a month before Sir Michael Foster had declared that he had complete confidence in the wisdom of the Joint Committee, and gave his cordial approval to its version of the Instructions. Now he had to eat his leek, which he did very gracefully. Sir George Goldie called upon Sir Michael Foster to second his motion. He at first hesitated, & whispered to his neighbours right and left, but then

[144]

stood up and boldly seconded the motion in a speech which satisfied the best friends of the Expedition. This decided all waverers, and the good ship went round on the right tack.

Of course Poulton and the out and out jobbers were furious. The conspiracy was exposed and thwarted. Poulton denounced the desertion of the R.S. Officials and declared he would write to the *Times*. There was a great deal of wrangling, Poulton up and down like a Jack in the box, the bird of prey and the scowling villain on their legs, Geikie and Wharton protesting, Sir George Goldie quietly dropping a little oil into the flames now and then. But the good ship was safe. The Motion was carried by an overwhelming majority, Poulton and the bird of prey entering their dissents on the minutes.

Grand Transformation Scene
Clown (Poulton)
Pantaloon (Wharton)
Harlequin (Goldie)
Columbine (Foster)
Villain (Tizard)
Bird of Prey (Buchanan)

Pas de deux of Harlequin and Columbine

But no more performances on this stage

Poulton fulfilled his threat. Norman Lockyer, the Editor of *Nature*, is always ready to do anything nasty, especially against the R.S. Officials, because he thinks he ought to be one himself. He inserted Poulton's long protest, and it also appeared in the *Times*. It is full of incorrect statements and untruths, but written from ignorance and dullness rather than from intention. The involved rigmarole would be unintelligible to outsiders. Its main object is to attack the R.S. Officials, especially Foster, for deserting science represented by Gregory. It divulged several confidential secrets, throwing light on some obscure points. When a certain class of persons falls out, a different class gets knowledge that would otherwise have been kept secret. Norman Lockyer tried to help with an article, declaring that if the R.S. Officials did not reply, judgment must go by default. The R.S. Officials wisely took no notice whatever, and the squib fizzled out.

The Royal Society nominated Lord Lindley, an eminent Judge, Lord Lister the ex-President, and Mr Kempe, R.S.

Treasurer, as its Members of the Select Committee. I nominated Sir George Goldie, Sir Leopold McClintock – the highest polar authority, and Mr Sutherland Mackenzie an able financier. Lord Lindley was Chairman, but there was no casting vote. There was practical unanimity, and the Committee never divided.

Select Committee

Royal Geographical Society	Royal Society
Sir George Goldie	Lord Lindley *(Chairman)*
Sir Leopold McClintock	Lord Lister
Mr Sutherland Mackenzie	Mr Kempe

The Select Committee met first on April 26th and again on April 28th. The document they worked upon was my Instructions of 1897 adopted by the Executive Committee on January 30th 1901. They took out all the mischievous alterations made by the Joint Committee and practically restored my paragraphs. Sir George Goldie, in the study of his brief, had taken Gregory's measure exactly. He knew that the Professor was elated by his supposed victory, and that he would resign if anything material was altered. It was necessary that he should be got rid of. It was quite impossible that he could now work harmoniously with Scott. On April 30th Pilot Goldie carried the main point, that the question of wintering should be left to the Commander. On May 6th a telegram was sent to Gregory at Melbourne, telling him that the Commander would have the option to winter, and that *he* would be under the orders of the Commander, asking if he agreed. His reply was 'No'. 'He could not be responsible for the scientific work under such an arrangement'.

This was what Goldie expected and intended. The R.S. Members were surprised. But all accepted the reply as a resignation.

Sir Michael Foster's love of meddling and intrigue was strong as ever. He sent a second telegram to Gregory, telling him that he had been elected a Fellow of the Royal Society and hoping he would reconsider. He again refused. Some other odd things were done. Longhurst was not summoned as clerk to the Select Committee, apparently to keep the proceedings from me. An R.S. clerk was employed quite unnecessarily. The Royal Society then sent in a bill against the Expedition of £35 for its unauthorized telegram, £5 for the clerk, and a bill for tea and bread and butter for the Select Committee. Gregory has cost seven hundred pounds from first to last, the result being nothing but squabbling, worry, and friction. The Expedition was well rid of him, even at that price.

The Select Committee completed its work admirably, and Lord Lindley sent the Instructions to the Presidents of the two Societies. They are practically the same as my draft of Instruction written in 1897. There is a longer paragraph about spring travelling which I wrote for Goldie; and another about a landing party (to please the Royal Society) in case the Commander should decide upon one which of course he would not do. The Instructions were signed by the two Presidents, and I gave them to Scott, on board the *Discovery*, on August 3d 1901.

It will be understood what an enormous weight of anxiety and worry was added to Scott's difficult work of fitting out the expedition, by this intolerable nuisance. It would have driven most men out of their senses. It had a visible effect on Scott: but he bore it all with most wonderful prudence, tact, and patience. The Royal Society, with its preposterous Joint Committee, has been a curse to the Expedition. Of course there is a moral to all this, and we can all be wise after the event. But things do not repeat themselves exactly in the same way. When Lord Linley's note came with the Instructions I drew a long breath of thankfulness, for all the tedious creatures with their obstructions and wearisome chatter were now dispersed.

Last scene of all. Solemn protest to Wharton to be placed on record in the archives of the Royal Society. Well! It is now *all* placed on record; a tale of dullness, intrigue, and spite; of malignity luckily mated with incapacity, finally and completely thwarted; thanks to 'The Pilot that weathered the storm'.

D

Final Reflections on the Vagaries of the Joint Committee

The story of this Joint Committee is so extraordinary that one naturally tries to explain it. Large Committees are nearly always useless, but some at least allow work to be done. The members of the Joint Committee were nearly all men of more or less ability, though some, probably the majority, were unpractical and narrow in their views, accustomed to work only in their own grooves. Still they were open to reason, and would doubtless have followed the lead of the officials of the two Societies, if they had been united.

The R.G.S. officials were perfectly sound, and without ulterior schemes of any kind. The R.S. Presidents were neutral and indifferent. Professor Rücker was a man of sense and with some force of character, but he was overwhelmed with other work, and was absent abroad during the most critical time. He would never have allowed things to drift into such a hopeless muddle. Mr Kempe, the Treasurer, was quite straight-forward. There remains Sir Michael Foster and, as from the nature of the case, the fault lies primarily with some leading official, this exhaustive process leaves it with him.

He must be a man of ability from being Professor of Physiology at Cambridge and Secretary of the Royal Society. He must be clever and popular from being Member for the London University. He is good natured, plausible, and agreeable, with rather a winning voice. But I judge him to be an inveterate jobber; and he cannot refrain from intrigue, and from playing people against each other, like chessmen. His proceedings were all in accordance with this estimate of his character. When I approached him in 1893 on the subject of an Antarctic Expedition, his first idea was to use it for the credit and honour of the Royal Society. Hence the R.S. deputation to the Government without my knowledge. When he agreed that the Societies should take joint action his idea was the same. He knew and cared nothing for the Antarctic Expedition, for he has never subscribed a farthing, nor has he ever been of the slightest use. But he thought some use could be made of it. His plan of a large Joint Committee was to relieve the R.S. Council of all responsibility; while getting as much credit as possible. He was neutral when the Hydrographers made their attack upon Scott, because he saw nothing to be got out of it; so he was glad when the matter was settled, and was even ready to help in preventing a dead lock. But the Gregory job was all due to Foster. He thought he saw in it a way of increasing the importance of himself and the Royal Society by giving preponderating influence to the civilians in the expedition. His was the Secret Caucus, and he has never been able to see that there was anything improper or unfair in that transaction. His was the springing of the mine upon us. His was the cordial approval of the alterations in the Instructions, which would have wrecked the expedition.

The resignation of the Admirals probably disturbed his peace of mind. The firm front of the R.G.S. Council and the request for a conference led him to think that the Gregory business might not have the consequences he intended. So he had no hesitation in agreeing to the neutrality of the R.S. Officials, which he soon converted into active help to us; coolly eating his words exactly a month after he had uttered them, and deserting his confederates.

The great body of the Joint Committee immediately went round with him or did not vote, showing how completely all the trouble had been caused by this one man. Others were very tiresome, and tried to do mischief, but without the countenance of a leading R.S. Official they would have had no following. The trouble was, therefore, primarily and mainly due to Sir Michael Foster. If he had refrained from intrigue, and had not put Wharton and Poulton on the Joint Committee, all would have been well, even with his unwieldy and heterogeneous machinery. There would have been no friction, and he would have gained his own object without endangering and nearly wrecking the Expedition.

Next to Foster the greatest enemy of the expedition has been Sir William Wharton, the Hydrographer. Of good family[47] and promising as a young naval officer, Wharton won the Beaufort Testimonial; and was Flag Lieutenant to Sir James Hope at Portsmouth. But he took to the surveying branch, and his naval career ended. He was appointed Hydrographer in 1885, and appeared to be a great improvement on his two immediate predecessors; and from that time he was on the R.G.S. Council. He was elected F.R.S. (1886) and has been on the R.S. Council (1888–89 and 1895–97). Wharton has been 19 years in civil employment on shore, as Hydrographer. He has no knowledge of polar work and its requirements, but expressed himself in favour of an Antarctic Expedition. Wharton is, however, an exceedingly difficult man to work with. He not only constantly finds fault, but worries things to death, wasting time over trifles to an extent which is exasperating. It is not in his nature to defer to any one however superior to himself in knowledge and experience; or to let any business be transacted without interminable and useless discussion.

To put such a man on the Joint Committee practically made work or progress impossible, and it was very improper and undesirable to put an Admiralty official on a Committee where appointments and other matters connected with his Department must be settled. For this we had to thank Sir Michael Foster.

[149]

Apart from the incessant wear and tear caused by Wharton at every meeting; he felt it his duty to make every effort to get the command of the Expedition for some one in his own Department. I have related the result, and the unreasonable persistency with which he pursued his object. It was the obstinacy of a weak and not very clever man.

He fortunately failed, but he did not forgive; and the course he subsequently took is indefensible. He had published his views. He had argued against the ship going near Victoria Land, and he had argued strongly against there being any landing party. Yet as soon as the Gregory job was matured, he at once joined in it, not only advocating the Victoria Land route, and a landing party under Gregory's command, but even drafting the paragraphs to be substituted for mine in the Instructions: and he took a prominent part in the subsequent irregular proceedings.

Wharton was able to do more mischief, because he had an official following, Tizard the Assistant Hydrographer, Creak and Field who were under Wharton departmentally; Nares and Aldrich who were long connected with the surveying branch. Thus he commanded five rotten boroughs, each with a vote.

The men on the Committee who had been in the *Challenger*, Nares, Aldrich, Tizard and Buchanan, set up a very untenable claim to be looked upon as Antarctic experts. The *Challenger* was among icebergs for ten days, and passed along the edge of the pack ice; but she never was *in* the pack, which alone could give Antarctic experience, and never sighted Antarctic land. It is true that Nares and Aldrich were also Arctic men and were versed in polar work; but the pretensions of Tizard and Buchanan are absurd. So much for the Hydrographic Clique.

The professorial clique was represented by Poulton. For him also we have to thank Sir Michael Foster. At that time they were close friends, and it appears, from Poulton's letter to the newspapers, that he had secret orders to push the supremacy of the civilian element by all means in his power. He had no object but to further Gregory's attempts to usurp authority, and he did this with some energy and much obstinacy. By representing that Gregory had been deceived and ill used he interested the three geologists on the Committee, Sir Archibald Geikie, Mr Teall, and Mr Blanford. The first of these, usually a quiet and cautious man, took a strong line and became a violent partisan, being guilty of the boorish rudeness I have described. But, after the first rush, the geologists rapidly cooled down and took a more sensible view. Buchanan, the bird of ill omen, continued to support all the extravagances of Poulton to the last.

There was this to be said for Poulton. He placed Gregory's interests and wishes first, and the good of the expedition nowhere; but he faithfully stuck to his friend. Others fell away or compromised, Foster ruined his scheme and deserted him, but he stood by his spiked guns – 'true to a worthless cause'. Poulton and Buchanan entered their silly protests on the Minutes.

All these people did what mischief they could. Wharton, Tizard, Field, Nares, Aldrich – and Poulton, Geikie, Teall, Buchanan, 9 of them. But of themselves they could have done no harm. It was the countenance of Sir Michael Foster which brought them forward. He was playing with them as if they were so many chessmen, and a very poor game he played. As soon as he became aware of that fact, he coolly upset the board, and there was an end of it. But it is a funny story! Poor Poulton may well complain that his friend 'did not play the game'. It barely deserves a place in an Appendix; and it is no part of the real history of the Expedition.

When two Societies act in concert to fit out an expedition the obviously proper course is to appoint a very small Committee consisting of the two Presidents, and the two Treasurers for the finance. They can call in experts to advise them on each point that arises respecting the plan of operations, instructions, ship, officers and men, outfit, scientific work &c; but should decide themselves. This is the only possible working plan, and probably there would never even be a division, as there never was in the late Select Committee. On this plan the joint Finance Committee is composed, and has worked admirably.

APPENDIX 1

[Instructions of the Joint Committee as finally overthrown at Markham's insistence. See Introduction.]

The Instructions to the Commander of the Expedition, as amended and finally approved by the Committee, read as follows:

(1) The Royal Society and the Royal Geographical Society, with the assistance of His Majesty's Government, have fitted out an expedition for scientific discovery and exploration in the Antarctic Regions, and have entrusted you with the command.

(2) The main objects of the Expedition are to determine, as far as possible, the nature, condition and extent of that portion of the South Polar lands which your expedition is able to reach; to make a magnetic survey in the southern regions to the south of the 40th parallel; and to carry on meteorological, oceanographic, geological, biological and physical investigations and researches.

(3) The Executive officers of the Expedition, including yourself, belong to the Naval service, and, having volunteered, their services have been placed at the disposal of the Societies by the Lords of the Admiralty. Their scientific work will be under your immediate control, and will include the magnetic and meteorological observations at sea, the astronomical observations, the surveying and charting, and the sounding operations.

(4) Associated with you there is a civilian scientific staff, with Dr. Gregory, D.Sc., Professor of Geology at the University of Melbourne, as Director, a copy of whose instructions are enclosed.

(5) In all questions connected with the scientific conduct of the Expedition you will consider Dr Gregory as your colleague, and on all these matters you will observe such consideration in respect to his wishes and suggestions as may be consistent with a due regard to the instructions under which you are acting, to the safe navigation of the ship, and to the comfort, health, discipline and efficiency of your crew. Those friendly relations and unreserved communications should be maintained between you, which will tend so materially to the success of an expedition

from which so many important results are looked for.

(6) As the scientific objects of the Expedition are manifold, some of them will come under the entire supervision of Professor Gregory and his staff; others will depend for their success on the joint co-operation of the naval and civil elements; while some will demand the undivided attention of yourself and your officers. Upon the harmonious working and hearty co-operation of all must depend the result of the Expedition as a whole.

(7) You are to consider the magnetic survey as one of the principal objects of the Expedition. The Expedition will be supplied with a complete set of magnetic instruments, both for observations at sea and on shore, instructions have been drawn up for their use by Captain Creak, R.N., and yourself and three of your officers have gone through a course of instruction at Deptford with Captain Creak and at Kew Observatory. The magnetic observatory on board the *Discovery* has been carefully constructed with a view to securing it from any proximity to steel or iron, and this has involved considerable expense and some sacrifice in other respects. We, therefore, impress upon you that the greatest importance is attached to the series of magnetic observations to be taken under your superintendence, and we desire that you will spare no pains to ensure their accuracy and continuity. The base station for your magnetic work will be at Melbourne: and that of the German Expedition will be at Kerguelen Island. The Government of the Argentine Republic has undertaken to establish a magnetic observatory at Staten Island. A secondary base station is to be established by you, if possible, in Victoria Land. You should endeavour to carry the magnetic survey from the Cape to Melbourne south of the 40th parallel, and from Melbourne across the Pacific to the meridian of Greenwich. It is also desired that you should observe along the tracks of Ross, in order to ascertain the magnetic changes that have taken place in the interval between the two voyages.

(8) The other primary object of the Expedition is geographical discovery and scientific exploration by sea and land, in two quadrants of the four into which the Antarctic regions are divided for convenience of reference, namely the Victoria and Ross Quadrants. It is desired that the extent of land should be ascertained by following the coast lines, that the depth and nature of the ice cap should be investigated, as well as the nature of the volcanic region, of the mountain ranges, and especially of any fossiliferous rocks.

(9) A German Expedition will start at the same time as the *Discovery*, and it is hoped that there will be cordial co-operation between the two expeditions as regards magnetic and meteorological observations, and in all other matters if opportunities offer for such co-operation. It is understood that the German Expedition will establish an observatory on Kerguelen Island, and will then proceed to explore the Enderby Quadrant, probably shaping a course south between the 70° E. and 80° E. meridians, with the object of wintering on the western side of Victoria Land, whence exploring sledge parties will be sent inland.

(10) A Swedish Expedition will probably undertake the Weddell Quadrant, and will establish a winter station on the eastern side of Graham's Island.

(11) You will see that the meteorological observations are regularly taken every two hours and, also, in accordance with a suggestion from the Berlin Committee, every day at Greenwich noon. It is very desirable that there should, if possible, be a series of meteorological observations to the south of the 75th parallel.

(12) Whenever it is possible, while at sea, deep sea sounding should be taken with serial temperatures, and samples of sea water at various depths are to be obtained, for physical and chemical analysis. Dredging operations are to be carried on as frequently as possible, and all opportunities are to be taken for making biological and geological collections.

(13) Instructions will be supplied for the various scientific observations; and the officers of the Expedition will be furnished with a manual, prepared and edited by Dr. George Murray, on similar lines and with the same objects as the Scientific Manual supplied to the Arctic Expedition of 1875.

(14) On leaving this country you are to proceed to Melbourne, touching at any port or ports on the way that you may consider it necessary or desirable to visit for supplies or repairs. Melbourne will be your base station. You will there fill up with live stock and other necessaries; and you will leave the port with three years' provisions on board, and fully supplied for wintering and for sledge travelling.

(15) You are to proceed at once to the edge of the pack and to force your vessel through it to the open water to the south. The pack is supposed to be closer in December than it has been found to be later in the season. But this is believed to depend rather on its position than on the time; and the great difference between a steamer and a sailing vessel perhaps makes up for any

difference in the condition of the pack.

(16) On reaching the south water, you will examine the coast of Lady Newnes' Bay to McMurdo Bay, with a view to finding a place which, in your opinion, is safe and suitable for the operations of landing, and having found one, you will land a party under the command of Professor Gregory, should he be satisfied with the suitability of the locality for winter quarters. The party having been landed, your subsequent movements during the remainder of the open season are to be independent of that party.

You will inform Professor Gregory as to the date at which he must be prepared to re-embark.

(17) The party should consist of Professor Gregory, Mr. Shackleton, Dr. Wilson and five men, including any who may have been specially engaged for the purpose by Professor Gregory, with the concurrence of the Commander, and should be supplied with dogs and sledges.

(18) The observations which would follow from the existence of the magnetic station on land will not only be of the greatest value themselves, but are necessary to obtaining the full value of the observations at sea; and magnetism as already stated, is one of the primary objects of the Expedition. Great importance also attaches to an examination of the ice mass covering the land, to a geological investigation of the volcanic regions, to inland explorations, to continuous meteorological observations, and to biological researches on shore. But, though you should bear in mind these important objects which will be attained by a landing party, in deciding what your actions should be if the difficulty of landing Professor Gregory and his party should prove to be very great, you should not lose sight of the fact that geographical exploration is another primary object of the Expedition.

(19) It is to be understood that the ship is not to winter in the Antarctic regions, if it can be avoided.

(20) No landing party is to be established on any other part of the coast than that between Lady Newnes' Bay and McMurdo Bay, as it is above all things essential that in case of accident the approximate position of the party should be known.

(21) Having established the station on shore, fully provided with all requisites for three years, or having examined the coast-line above indicated as thoroughly as practicable, and that examination having convinced you that a party could not be landed as that time in accordance with the foregoing instructions, you are, if the season be not too far advanced, to

turn your attention to exploration, either of the Coast of Victoria Land, west of Cape Adare, or to the eastward of the ice cliffs discovered by Sir James Ross.

(22) When it is so late as to endanger the freedom of your ship, you will proceed north of the pack, and carry out magnetic observations, with sounding and dredging over as many degrees of longitude, and as far south as possible, so long as the season and your coal permit.

(23) Presuming that you return to Melbourne in April, 1902, it is not probable that any advantage would be gained by an attempt to carry out further observations in high latitudes.

For your further movements you will receive instructions at Melbourne from England.

(24) Sub-Lieut. Armitage, R.N.R., has been appointed second in command and navigator to the Expedition. This officer has had experience in the work of taking astronomical, magnetic, and meteorologial observations during three polar winters. He has also acquired experience in sledge travelling, and in the driving and management of dogs. You will, no doubt, find his knowledge and experience of great use.

(25) You are to leave full details of your intentions with regard to the places where you will deposit records, and the course you will adopt, as well as particulars of your arrangements for the possible need of retreat, so that in case of accident to the ship, or detention, we shall be able to use our best endeavours to carry out your wishes in this respect.

You will exercise the greatest economy in your coal, using your sails as much as possible, and remembering never to allow your coal supply to fall below the quantity sufficient for the requirements of wintering, should your ship be unfortunately beset.

(26) In an enterprise, the nature of which we have explained to you, much must be left to the discretion and judgment of the commanding officer, and we fully confide in your combined energy and prudence for the successful issue of a voyage which will command the attention of scientific men throughout the civilised world. At the same time we desire you constantly to bear in mind our anxiety for the health, comfort and the safety of the officers and men entrusted to your care.

(27) While employed on this service you are to take every opportunity of acquainting us with your progress and your requirements.

(28) In the unfortunate event of any fatal accident happening

to yourself, or of your inability, from sickness or any other cause, to carry out these instructions, the command of the ship and of the Expedition will devolve on Lieutenant Armitage, who is hereby directed to assume command, and to execute such part of these instructions as have not been already carried out at the time of his assuming command. In the event of a similar accident to Lieutenant Armitage, the command is to devolve on the executive officer next in seniority on the Articles, and so on in succession.

It is to be understood that all collections, and all logs, journals, charts, drawings, photographs, observations, and scientific data are to be considered as the joint property of the Councils of the two Societies, to be disposed of as may be decided by them. Before the final return of the Expedition, you are to demand from the Naval Staff all such data, which are to be sealed up and delivered to the two Presidents, or dealt with as they may direct. The Director of the civilian Scientific Staff will be similarly responsible for the journals, collections, &c., of the officers under his control. You and the other members of the Expedition will not be at liberty to publish independent narratives until six months after the issue of the official narrative.

(29) The *Discovery* is the first ship that has ever been built expressly for scientific purposes in these kingdoms. It is an honour to receive the command of her; but we are impressed with the difficulty of the enterprise which has been entrusted to you, and with the serious character of your responsibilities. The Expedition is an undertaking of national importance; and science cannot fail to benefit from the efforts of those engaged in it. You may rely upon our support on all occasions, and we feel assured that all on board the *Discovery* will do their utmost to further the objects of the Expedition.

(Signed)   President R.S.
President R.G.S.

The Instructions to the Director of the Civilian Scientific Staff, as amended and finally approved by the Committee (including the paragraphs passed finally at the Meeting held on February 12), read as follows:-

(1) The Councils of the Royal Society and the Royal Geographical Society have approved your appointment as

Director of the Civilian Scientific Staff of their Antarctic Expedition.

(2) You will have control and superintendence in all scientific investigations not specially entrusted to the Commander, and will direct the scientific work of the gentlemen who have been appointed to assist you.

(3) The names of the gentlemen associated with you, who have been approved by yourself and by the Commander of the Expedition, are as follows:-

> (1) Mr. Hodgson (*Biologist*).
>
> (2) Mr. Shackleton (*Physicist*).

The services of the two medical officers will be at your disposal for scientific work when not engaged on the work of their own department, namely Dr. Koettlitz (*Botanist*), and Dr. Wilson (*Zoologist*).

(4) The main objects of the Expedition are to determine, as far as possible, the nature, condition, and extent of that portion of the south polar lands which it is able to reach; to make a magnetic survey in the southern regions to the south of the 40th parallel; and to carry on meteorological, oceanographic, geological, biological, and physical investigations and researches.

(5) The Commander of the Expedition, a copy of whose Instructions will be supplied to you, has been directed, if he can find a place which is safe and suitable for the operation of landing, to land you with a party, of which you will be in charge, for the purpose of wintering, and you will superintend the magnetic and meteorological observations at the land station, which will be, especially the former, of primary importance in connection with similar observations carried on in the ship.

(6) With the magnetic survey, the other primary object of the expedition is geographical discovery and scientific exploration by sea and land, in two quadrants of the four into which the Antarctic regions are divided for convenience of reference, namely, the Victorian and Ross Quadrants. It is desired that the extent and configuration of the land should be ascertained by explorations inland or coastwise; that the depth, condition, and nature of the ice-cap should be investigated, as well as the nature of the volcanic region, of the mountain ranges, and especially of any fossiliferous rocks.

(7) You will see that meteorological observations at your land station are taken regularly every two hours, and also, in accordance with a suggestion from the Berlin Committee, every day at Greenwich noon.

(8) The ship will proceed to Melbourne, which will be the base station, and where you will join. The ship will leave Melbourne with three years' provisions on board, and fully supplied for wintering and sledge travelling.

(9) The ship will proceed at once to the edge of the pack and endeavour to force her way through to the open water to the south, and carry out the further instructions given to the Commander.

(10) The Commander of the Expedition has been instructed to communicate freely with you on all matters connected with the scientific objects of the Expedition, and, as far as possible, to meet your views and wishes in connection with them. The Councils of the two Societies feel assured that you will co-operate and act in concert with him, with a view, as far as possible, to secure the success of an enterprise which it is hoped will be attended with important results in the various branches of science which it is intended to investigate.

(11) It is to be understood that all collections, and all logs, journals, charts, drawings, photographs, observations and scientific data are to be considered as the joint property of the two Societies, to be disposed of as may be decided by them. Before the final return of the Expedition, you are to demand from the staff under your control all such data, which are to be sealed up and delivered to the two Presidents, or dealt with as they may direct. On the return of the Expedition, it is hoped you will be able to superintend the distribution of specimens to specialists approved of by the two Councils or their representatives, and possibly to edit the resulting reports. It is understood that the Melbourne University will have the first set of duplicate specimens. You will also be expected to contribute a report on the scientific results of the expedition for the official narrative. As it may be desirable during the progress of the voyage that any new scientific discoveries should be at once made known in the interests of science, you are authorised to use your judgment as to the time and method of accomplishing this object, and of communicating such scientific information as you may judge fitting to learned societies or scientific journals.

(12) You and other members of the Expedition, will not be at liberty to publish independent narratives until six months after the issue of the official narrative.

(13) Should any vacancies in the scientific staff occur after the Expedition has sailed from England, you may, with the concurrence of the Commander, make such arrangements as

you think desirable to fill the vacancy, should no one have been appointed from England.

(Signed) President R.S.
President R.G.S.

APPENDIX 2

[From *Nature* Vol. 64, 23 May, 1901]
The National Antarctic Expedition

We print below a letter which Prof. Poulton has addressed to the Fellows of the Royal Society in regard to the Antarctic expedition. In it he gives a history of the circumstances which have caused Prof. J. W. Gregory to resign the leadership of the scientific staff. The reason for this, to follow the Professor's words, is that since he left England in February changes have been made in his position in regard to the naval commander of the expedition which deprived him of any guarantee that the scientific work would not be subordinated to naval adventure, 'an object admirable in itself, but not the one for which I understood this expedition to be organised.' The history of the negotiations before and since the beginning of the present year – the date of the letter in which these words occur – show that when Prof. Gregory accepted the leadership of the scientific work (late in 1899), much stress had been laid on the scientific aspect of the expedition, and that the alterations made since the beginning of the present year have increased the authority of the naval commander.

At a special meeting of the Royal Society in February 1898, when the advantages of an Antarctic expedition were fully discussed, Sir John Murray, in an admirable summary of matters requiring further study, enumerated not only the depth, the deposits and the biology of the South Polar Ocean, but also the meteorology, magnetism, geology, and ice-sheet of the region; and laid special stress on the importance of landing a party to remain over at least one winter in order to study the latter points. Dr. Neumayer, Sir Joseph Hooker, Sir A. Geikie and the Duke of Argyll all enlarged on the importance of one or more of the second group. The same were mentioned by members of the deputation, which Mr. Balfour received in June 1899, and in his reply he acknowledged their importance. It is, therefore, not surprising that Prof. Gregory expected the leader of the scientific staff to be allowed a very free hand, and it certainly seems that the negotiations, described by Prof.

Poulton, have tended to deprive him of initiative and to place him more completely under the authority of the naval commander. Yet this expedition will afford a great opportunity not only for geographical discovery, but also for increasing scientific knowledge; and for some most important things in the latter a prolonged stay on land is absolutely necessary. Chief among these, in addition to magnetic work, are the following:- The Antarctic land is covered by an ice-sheet greater than that of Greenland, and certainly not less than even the one which some glacialists assert to have formerly existed in Northern Europe. In that land also, as in no other place, we have a chance of obtaining the key to some curious problems in the zoology and botany, past and present, of other continental masses in the southern hemisphere. For both these problems a prolonged residence is required, and an expert who, like Prof. Gregory, is as familiar with ice and its work as he is with palaeontological questions.

We may hope then that those representatives of science on the Joint Antarctic Committee whom Prof. Poulton accuses will be able to demonstrate that he is wrong and Prof. Gregory needlessly apprehensive, that Commander Scott possesses such experience in Polar exploration and has such familiarity with the branches of science which we have mentioned as to warrant a man of Prof. Gregory's age and standing in placing himself absolutely under his orders, and that the *Discovery* is a King's ship in so full and real a sense that such entire subjection, even to signing articles, is imperative. Until their explanation is before us we cannot be expected to express a final opinion on the merits of the dispute, and this we shall no doubt obtain very shortly; for those whom Prof. Poulton has accused of running the risk of subordinating scientific investigation to geographical discovery can hardly afford to let judgment go by default.

To the Fellows of the Royal Society

The resignation of the man who is, before all others, fitted to be the Scientific Leader of the National Antarctic Expedition will lead the Fellows of the Society to expect some statement of the causes which have produced a result so disastrous to the interests of science. The following statement gives an account of the efforts which have been made to prevent the injury which has occurred.

In the autumn of 1899 Captain Tizard, F.R.S., and I were

[162]

appointed as the representatives of the Council of the Royal Society on an Antarctic Executive Committee of four, Sir Clements Markham (Chairman) and Sir R. Vesey Hamilton being the representatives of the Royal Geographical Society's Council. Our functions were defined under various heads in a printed form previously agreed upon. No. 2 instructed us to submit a programme of the Expedition for approval to the Joint Antarctic Committee (consisting of sixteen representatives of each Council), 'such a programme to include (*a*) A general plan of the operations of the Expedition, including instructions to the Commander, so far as this can be laid down beforehand. (*b*) The composition of the executive and scientific staff to be employed, the duties, preparation and accommodation for, and pay of, the several members.' No. 4 instructed us 'To make the appointments of the several members of the executive and scientific staff, subject to the final approval of the Joint Committee.' The word 'civilian' was nowhere employed. The four members of the Executive Committee were placed on the Joint Committee and all Sub-Committees.

Before the first meeting of the Executive Committee Captain Tizard and I were seen by Prof. Rücker, who informed us that one of the first points which the Council of the Royal Society desired us to raise was the relation in power and status between the Commander and the Scientific Leader. In the German Expedition, which was to start about the same time, the Scientific Director had absolute power, and we were asked to consider the possibility of such an arrangement in the English Expedition.

At one of our first meetings, I think the very first, I raised this question and supported the German arrangement. The other three members, who were all naval experts, convinced me that English law required the Captain to be supreme in all questions relating to the safety of his ship and crew. Since that time I have never disputed this point, but always maintained that the scientific chief should be head of the scientific work of all kinds, including the geographical, and that the captain should be instructed to carry out his wishes so far as they were consistent with the safety of ship and crew.

We then considered the appointment of Scientific Leader and decided to nominate Prof. J. W. Gregory, then of the British Museum of Natural History. In suggesting his name to my colleagues I was influenced by his proved success in organisation and in the management of men in a most difficult expedition (British East Africa in 1893), by the wide grasp of science which enabled him to bring back valuable observations and collections in so many departments. His ice experience in Spitzbergen and Alpine regions was also of the highest importance, together with the fact that his chief subject was Geology, a science which pursued in the Antarctic Continent would almost certainly yield results of especial significance. In addition to all these qualifications Prof. Gregory's wide and varied knowledge of the earth rendered his opinion as to the lines of work which would be most likely to lead to marked success extremely valuable in such an Expedition. No one was more competent to state the probable structure of the Antarctic Continent and its relation to that of the earth. This opinion of Prof. Gregory's qualifications for the position of scientific leader of an Antarctic expedition is I know widely held among British scientific men. In their wide combination and united as they are to tried capacity as a leader they are unique, and an expedition with Prof. Gregory for its scientific chief, with as free a hand as English law would permit, was bound to yield great results.

The Committee deputed me to ask Prof. Gregory if he would consent to be nominated. In doing so I carefully explained that he could not have the full powers of the German scientific leader. He consented to consider the offer favourably, but wished for a more definite statement of his position and powers, and for a programme of the Expedition. Shortly after this he was appointed Professor of Geology at Melbourne, and left England. On the voyage he wrote a long letter to the Executive Committee (dated January 19, 1900), which he posted to me at Port Said. In it he said, 'I have heard so many rumours as to what is wanted, that I cannot be sure whether I correctly understand the views and wishes of the Executive Committee: I therefore write mainly for the sake of correction, so that I may avoid any misstatements in communicating with the Council of Melbourne University, when the proposal from the Committee reaches me.' The plan drafted by Prof. Gregory in this letter included the provision of a landing party with house, observing huts, dog-stable, &c., and he argued that its organisation should be placed 'in the hands of the scientific staff,' but that, under any circumstances, the Scientific Leader should have the opportunity of controlling a small independent party on land. This letter was read by all the members of the Executive Committee, and, on June 15, at the close of the meeting, the Secretary despatched a cable to Prof. Gregory containing the information 'Your letter of January 19 has been received and approved.' As soon as Prof.

Gregory received this he sent a decoded copy to Sir Clements Markham, who did not correct it. Indeed, at this period Sir Clements Markham frequently expressed opinions which implied that he contemplated the establishment of a landing party independent of the ship. Prof. Gregory applied for and received from the Council of Melbourne University permission to take the appointment on the lines of his letter of January 19.

Prof. Gregory's name was very warmly received by the Joint Committee and he was appointed Scientific Head on February 14, 1900: the words 'Formally appointed, wire when fully able to decide,' being cabled to him a few days later by Sir Clements Markham.

Lieutenant Robert F. Scott, Torpedo Lieutenant of H.M.S. *Majestic*, was appointed Commander of the Expedition by the Joint Committee on May 25, 1900.

In June 1900 my attention was called to a statement in the Press describing Prof. Gregory as 'Head of the Civilian Scientific Staff.' Feeling confident that the word 'civilian' was not employed in the resolution accepted by the Joint Committee I wrote to Sir Clements Markham on the subject. In his absence the Secretary replied, 'The words "Head of the Civilian Scientific Staff" are the exact words of the resolution passed by the Joint Committee appointing Prof. Gregory, and I know Sir Clements himself was very anxious to have the word 'civilian' in, so that no difficulty might arise between Prof. Gregory and the Commander of the Expedition, since the Civilians would not be the only scientific men on board.' The word 'civilian' does certainly occur in the minutes of the meeting. On the other hand, Sir Clements Markham was not present on that occasion (February 14, 1900); the word 'civilian' did not occur in the instructions issued to the Executive Committee, and was not used in my letter to Sir Clements (February 15) describing the result of the meeting and asking him to cable. The words I used, 'leader of the Scientific Staff,' were not commented upon in his reply (February 16), stating that the cable should be sent. The word 'civilian' was not used by Dr. W. T. Blanford writing to convey the unanimous recommendation of the Geological Sub Committee that Prof. Gregory should be 'chief of the Scientific Staff of the Expedition.' Prof. Herdman, who seconded the resolution on February 14, and I who proposed it, both remember the words 'Scientific Leader of the Expedition.' I have not been able to recover a copy of the notice convening the meeting, in which the agenda were put down. It would, however, have been unreasonable for the Joint Committee to have accepted the word 'civilian' when it had no information before it which justified the expectation that naval officers would be lent by the Admiralty.

At the meeting of the British Association at Bradford I explained the situation to Prof. Rücker, who agreed with me that it was full of danger, on account of the reasons alleged for the use of the word 'civilian,' viz. in order to discriminate between the science under Prof. Gregory and that under the Commander. He agreed with me that the coordination of all the science of the Expedition ought to be in the hands of the scientific chief who had been selected because his reputation was a guarantee that all interests would be properly looked after. Sir Michael Foster, to whom I mentioned the matter at a later date, quite agreed with this opinion, but was unwilling to contest the use of the term 'civilian.' Furthermore, when I raised the question at a meeting of the Representatives of the Royal Society on the Joint Committee, it appeared that the term was actually preferred by certain influential naval authorities who were present, so that it was impossible to resist it without dividing those who desired to give Prof. Gregory such a measure of freedom of action as he was prepared to accept.

At the meeting (November 20, 1900) of the Joint Committee following the conversations with Prof. Rücker and Sir Michael Foster, a Report from the Executive Committee and Submission and Estimate from Captain Scott were read and received, with certain modifications. I indicated to the Secretaries of the Royal Society, who were sitting opposite to me, that this was a favourable opportunity to raise the question of the powers of the Scientific Director over the whole of the science of the Expedition. They were, however, unwilling to do so, hoping, I believe, that all difficulties would be smoothed away by personal negotiations between Captain Scott and Prof. Gregory, who was expected home in a fortnight.

For nearly two months these negotiations proceeded between Prof. Gregory on the one side and Captain Scott and Sir Clements Markham on the other, and between Sir Clements Markham and me.

The principles held were irreconcilable, and it only remained to appeal to the Joint Committee for a decision.

On January 9, 1901, Prof. Gregory wrote to Prof. Rücker explaining the failure of the negotiations, and on January 28 he addressed a letter to the Royal Society's Representatives on the

Joint Committee, from which I select the following paragraphs:

'I landed at Liverpool on December 5, and went straight to Dundee to meet Captain Scott, and showed him a copy of my letter of January 19 [1900]. As he returned it to me next day without comment I believed that he understood and accepted the general conditions therein stated. On January 7, in order to settle the exact terms of our mutual relations, I submitted to Captain Scott a draft of the instructions I expected to receive from the Joint Committee, and which I had previously shown to Prof. Poulton. To my surprise Sir Clements Markham and Captain Scott expressed disapproval of these instructions, practically on the ground that there could be only one leader of the Expedition, and that that leader must be Captain Scott.

'My colleagues and myself were characterised as civilian scientific experts, accompanying the expedition to undertake investigations in those branches of science with which the ship's officers were unfamiliar, and it was proposed, that to maintain Captain Scott's complete control, all the scientific men should be required to sign articles.

'According to this theory the position of the scientific staff is accessory and subordinate. The contentions of Sir Clements Markham and Captain Scott would completely alter the position which I was invited to take and which alone I am prepared to accept. Were I to accompany the expedition on those terms there would be no guarantee to prevent the scientific work from being subordinated to naval adventure, an object admirable in itself, but not the one for which I understood this expedition to be organised.'

The Executive Committee met on January 30 and drafted instructions on lines approved by Sir Clements Markham. They were opposed by my colleague Captain Tizard, but in my absence through illness were passed by two votes to one.

A few days later the draft instructions were considered by the Royal Society's Representatives, who appointed Sir Joseph Hooker, Sir William Wharton and Sir Archibald Geikie to suggest amendments. They carefully considered the draft and suggested several alterations, the most important of these being the instructions to the commander, (1) not to winter in the ice, (2) to establish between two named points on the coast a landing party with three years' stores, under the control of Prof. Gregory.

The Royal Society's Representatives again met and unanimously approved these amendments, which were submitted together with the draft instructions to the meeting of the Joint Committee on February 8. The Representatives of the Royal Geographical Society objected that they had not had the same opportunity of considering the instructions at a separate meeting, and that the amendments were sprung upon them. The meeting was accordingly adjourned until February 12, the very day before Prof. Gregory sailed. During the prolonged discussion which took place the authorities on magnetism were unanimous in affirming that a station on land was essential in order to obtain the full value of the observations made on the ship.

Sir Clements Markham threatened that the Council of the R.G.S. would not accept the amended instructions, whereupon Sir Michael Foster drew attention to the letter which Sir Clements had written at the time when the Joint Committee was proposed.

The amendments were finally approved by 16 votes to 6, and Sir Archibald Geikie and I were deputed to explain to Prof. Gregory, who was in attendance, that he was to be landed in control of a small party, if a safe and suitable place could be found, and to ask if he would accept these conditions. We reported his consent to the meeting, which was then adjourned for the consideration of other details.

Two of the Representatives of the R.G.S., Sir Anthony Hoskins and Sir Vesey Hamilton, resigned shortly afterwards, explaining that they could not agree with the action of the Committee. The R.G.S. had however the right, which it subsequently exercised, of appointing new members.

At the adjourned meeting, on February 19, the question of the ship wintering was discussed at length. Those who had practical experience of the Antarctic urged us strongly not to take the responsibility of permitting the ship to winter in the ice. Sir Joseph Hooker's statement of the danger was especially impressive, and the meeting decided in accordance with his opinion.

At the same meeting Major L. Darwin proposed to modify the conditions accepted by Prof. Gregory, by adding to them the additional consideration that he should only be landed if the time of the ship should not be too greatly diverted from geographical exploration. I protested strongly against any modification at this stage. Sir Michael Foster opposed me, and, after the close of the meeting, there was a somewhat sharp though friendly expression of conflicting opinions, he maintaining that there should be 'give and take,' I that we were already pledged to Prof. Gregory, that the arrangement was as it stood a compromise – the minimum Prof. Gregory would accept – by no means the one which scientific men, not belonging to the Navy, would have preferred.

At that meeting Major Darwin did not succeed, but his suggestion in somewhat different words was again brought forward at the next meeting on March 5. Just before the meeting Sir Archibald Geikie told me that he intended to support the proposed changes 'in the interests of peace,' and that Mr. Teall, and Mr. George Murray, Prof. Gregory's representative, also approved them. Resistance was hopeless; I could only protest against any alteration of the conditions offered and accepted, requesting that my name and the names of those who agreed with me (Mr. J. Y. Buchanan and Captain Tizard) should be recorded.

I wrote to Prof. Gregory a full account of what had happened, carefully explaining that his representative and many of his friends supported the changes, that I had confidence that the proposal was made to enable the Geographical Society to accept the instructions and that it was not intended to prevent and I believed would not prevent his being landed.

In spite of the incorporation of Major Darwin's changes the R.G.S. Council refused to accept the instructions, but addressed a letter signed by their President, dated March 18, to the members of the Joint Committee stating that they were compelled, 'as trustees for the money subscribed, through their Society and for the funds voted by their Society, to regard the above scientific objects [viz. those to be carried out by a landing party] as subsidiary to the two primary objects of the Expedition – namely, exploration and magnetic observations.' In view of the unanimous witness of all experts that the landing party was *essential* for full success in the magnetic work this statement is sufficiently remarkable.

The letter went on to inform us that the President, Sir Leopold McClintock, and Sir George Goldie had interviewed the officers of the Royal Society and had reported to the R.G.S. Council which now suggested that the Joint Committee should recommend a small Committee of six, three to be appointed by each Council, to deal finally with the Instructions. The Council of the R.G.S. agreed to accept the decision of this Committee provided the Council of the Royal Society agreed to do the same.

It has been stated in various directions that the Geographical Society produced new evidence (based upon the experience of

[169]

Borchgrevink and the intentions of the German leader) which had not been laid before the Joint Committee, and thus induced the officers of the Royal Society to agree to a new Committee. To this it may be replied that these sources of information had been open to the Joint Committee, and that, if anything new had arisen, it was reasonable to refer it to the old Committee rather than to a new one appointed *ad hoc*. Furthermore, the letter of the Royal Geographical Society referred to above clearly indicated that the real intention was to escape from the conditions proposed to and accepted by the scientific leader.

The Joint Committee met on April 26, and was addressed in favour of the course proposed by the R.G.S. Council by Sir George Goldie. Nothing was said which could diminish the conviction that the R.G.S. Council and that of the R.S. in weakly consenting to nominate a fresh Committee had struck a disastrous blow at all future cooperation between scientific bodies in this country.

What reply could the Officers make if they were asked to advise the Council of the Royal Society to cooperate with that of the Royal Geographical Society on any future occasion?

I felt justified in asking what guarantee was there that the Council of the Royal Geographical Society would accept the finding of the Committee of six, when it had refused to accept that of a Committee which included all the officers and almost every expert in Arctic and Antarctic Exploration from both Societies. In reply Sir Michael Foster, in spite of the promise of firmness held out by his attitude on February 12, when Sir Clements Markham threatened that his Council would repudiate the finding of the Joint Committee, maintained that they had only acted within their rights, and that the Royal Society Council claimed the right to do the same if it had not agreed with the decision.

At this point it will be convenient to give a list of the Representatives of the Royal Society on the Joint Antarctic Committee, the Representatives of the Royal Geographical Society being equally significant in relation to the Council of their own Society. They are the President, the Treasurer, the Senior Secretary, the Junior Secretary, Mr. A. Buchan, Mr. J. Y. Buchanan, Captain Creak, Sir J. Evans, Sir A. Geikie, Prof. Herdman, Sir J. D. Hooker, Prof. Poulton, Mr. P. L. Sclater, Mr. J. J. H. Teall, Captain Tizard, and Admiral Sir W. J. L. Wharton.

If the reports of Joint Committees of such magnitude and

weight are to be thrown over with the approval of the Councils of both Societies because a majority of one Council does not agree with the conclusions, men will rightly hesitate before consenting to devote an immense amount of time and trouble to the work of the Society, and the efficiency of the Royal Society will be greatly diminished.

The considerations set forth above indicate the future injuries which are likely to be inflicted on our Society by this surrender. At the meeting on April 26 I was more concerned with the immediate and pressing injury, and therefore urged that the Royal Society was a trustee for the interests of science and that we had pledged ourselves to secure certain powers to the Scientific Director, that it was better the Expedition should not start (a contingency contemplated as possible by Sir George Goldie, but not a serious danger, I believe, even though the Royal Society had stood firm and appealed to the Government, not on the subject-matter in dispute, but on the refusal of the Royal Geographical Society to work with the recognised methods of cooperation) than that the Royal Society should betray its trust, that the Fellows of the Society would not support the Officers in thus yielding to the Royal Geographical Society, and that I should feel bound to explain my position to the Society. Sir Archibald Geikie and Mr. J. Y. Buchanan also strongly objected to the surrender, which was then confirmed by a large majority of those present.

We were told by Sir George Goldie about the three Representatives of the Royal Geographical Society on the new Committee would be Sir Leopold McClintock, Mr. Mackenzie, and Sir George himself; by Sir Michael Foster that the Royal Society Council would appoint three non-experts, viz. Lord Lister, Lord Lindley and the Treasurer, who could pronounce without bias upon the whole of the evidence. My colleague, Captain Tizard, with whom I had worked with the most complete sympathy and agreement through the whole course of the negotiations, supported the formation of the new Committee because of Sir Michael's assurance that all evidence would be sifted and because of his faith in the validity of the evidence he had to give. Others probably voted in the affirmative for the same reason.

Without asking for evidence from Sir Joseph Hooker, Sir W. Wharton, Sir George Nares, Sir A. Geikie, Captain Creak, Captain Tizard, or Mr. Buchanan, the new Committee proceeded to cable to Melbourne the modifications which have led Prof. Gregory to resign.

In bringing a condensed account of the negotiations before the Fellows of the Royal Society I desire to call attention to certain special difficulties which the Society has had to encounter in the struggle.

(1) The fact that nearly the whole of the money voluntarily subscribed was obtained through members of the Geographical Society and from its funds.

(2) The fact that Sir Clements Markham, President of the Royal Geographical Society, a man of remarkable energy, resource and resolution, was the chief antagonist of the amendments passed by the Joint Committee.

(3) The fact that the Junior Secretary and Sir John Evans were absent from England during the most critical period.

(4) Prof. Gregory's appointment to the Chair at Melbourne, involving his absence from England during a large part of the negotiations.

Making all allowance for these difficulties, I believe that the majority of the Fellows will consider that the claims of the Scientific Chief in an Expedition undertaken to do scientific work have not received from the Royal Society that unflinching, undivided and resolute support which they would have expected and desired.   EDWARD B. POULTON.
Oxford, May 15.

NOTES

INTRODUCTION

1. A. H. Markham, *The life of Sir Clements R. Markham, K.C.B., F.R.S.* London, John Murray, 1917, pp. vii–viii.
2. Roland Huntford, *Scott and Amundsen*. London, Hodder and Stoughton, 1979, p. 128.
3. H. R. Mill, *The record of the Royal Geographical Society, 1830–1930*. London, RGS, 1930, p. 163 (copyright RGS).
4. Ibid, pp. 163–4.
5. Huntford, 1979, p. 128.
6. 'The National Antarctic Expedition 1901–03 and the Royal Geographical Society: a collection of unpublished documents'. Scott Polar Research Institute (SPRI) Manuscript 367/23, item 19.
7. SPRI Manuscript 367/23, item 19.
8. SPRI Manuscript 367/23, item 21.
9. J. W. Gregory, correspondence with family and colleagues, 1899–1901. SPRI Manuscript 1329.
10. SPRI Manuscript 1329.
11. SPRI Manuscript 367/23, item 32.
12. SPRI Manuscript 367/23, item 35.

PERSONAL NARRATIVE

1. The British Arctic Expedition, 1875–6, Captain G. S. Nares (see introduction).
2. Nansen's Arctic Ocean drift expedition on *Fram*, 1893–6.
3. Markham's footnote:
   At that time Scott was 16, Armitage 19, Royds 10, Barne 7, Shackleton 10, Skelton 12, Ferrar 6. I had studied Ross's narrative with care, in August 1850.
4. Markham's footnote:
   He suggested Sabrina Id as a good position for observing the transit.
5. Markham's footnote:
   Spenser's 'Faerie Queene'. Book II. Iv. Verse 42. Line 3. Glossary – 'derring doe' = bold deeds, chivalry, manhood.
6. Albert Hastings Markham.
7. Roland Huntford (*op. cit.*, p. 130) disputes this version of events, implying that Markham doctored the record to provide a better story. In fact, he informs, us, Tom Smyth was the 'star' of Markham's diaries at the time and was his favourite for command of the expedition.
8. The Jackson-Harmsworth Polar Expedition, leader Frederick George Jackson, 1894–7; explored the Zemlya Frantsa-Iosifa archipelago.
9. Markham's footnote:
   McClintock, Vesey Hamilton, Colomb, Markham, Lord Charles Beresford.

10. Markham's footnote:

<pre>
                    Dr. William Markham D.C.L.
                       (Archbishop of York)
        ┌──────────────────────────────────┐
 William Markham Esq   Countess of Mansfield
        │   │
 Revd. David F. Markham   Marchioness of Hertford
        │   │
 Sir Clements Markham K.C.B.   Lady Constance Barne
                                        │
                                  Lieut. Michael Barne R.N.
</pre>

11. Shackleton subsequently fell out of favour with Markham, mainly for organizing his *Nimrod* expedition to the Antarctic, 1907–9, which Markham saw as a threat to Scott's plans for a second expedition. Consequently, all favourable references to Shackleton in this passage have at some later date been crossed out or amended. Thus, this whole first sentence has been changed to 'Scott appointed Ernest Shackleton as third executive officer. Lower down, the word 'thorough' in 'thorough seaman' is crossed out, and 'He is a steady, high principled young man . . .' is amended to 'He seemed a steady young man. . . .'

12. Markham's footnote:
Meeting 26 April. Sir Clements in the Chair, McClintock, Nares, Markham, Aldrich, Egerton, W. E. Smith
To be built of wood, following line of old *Discovery*.
Laboratories.
43 souls, amount of provisions, accommodation
400 H.P. coal capacity 335 tons (old Discovery 190)
150 increased to
Double topsails
Two bladed lifting screw
Shipping and unshipping rudder

13. Markham's footnote:
30 June. Increased length agreed to, of 10 ft.

14. Throughout the narrative Markham changes repeatedly from the correct spelling 'Lyttelton' to 'Lyttleton'.

15. Two lines here are rubbed out, with the marginal note: 'Else did not go out'; presumably a reference to the Steward Edward Else who was appointed to the expedition but did not sail.

16. Markham's footnote:

Available ships in Norway

	Gross Tonnage	Length	Width	Depth	
Morgenen	451	140ft	31ft	16½	Very strong ship. Repairs last year on hull & engine
Niord	522	152	30½	17½	Built 1886. Strong good ship. Slightly wormed. *Not for sale*
Samson	506	148	31	17	Very strong, good ship. Keel & bottom badly wormed. *Not for sale*
Viking	586	152	32	17½	Built 1882. Very good ship, but not free from being worm eaten. *Not for sale.*
Capella					Leaks very badly. Repairs required. Worn out
Vega					Wants repairs and new boiler.

Hecla (bought by Bruce), *Belgica*, *Antarctica* (bought by Swedes).

Terra Nova (Newfoundland) sold, *Nova Zembla* too small, last in Davis Strait
1902
Eclipse (Built at Aberdeen) *not for sale* too small
Active
Balaena⎫ *Built at*   . *Worn out, & too small. Not for sale.*
Diana ⎭

17. See Appendix 1.
18. Markham's footnote:
    £16 a month
19. Markham's footnote:
    Special course of surveying as a Torpedo Lieutenant. He wrote the whole
    section on mining survey for the Torpedo Manual, and suggested all the
    instruments to be used. The matter was put into his hands when he joined
    the *Defiance*. He had a thorough knowledge of the principles of surveying
    and of surveying instruments as well as of electricity and magnetism.
20. Markham has crossed out this entry and added the remark 'Came back
    March 1903'.
21. Entry crossed out, with remark 'Ran at Lyttelton. Objectionable'.
22. Entry crossed out, with remark 'Killed. Fell from aloft'.
23. Entry crossed out, with remark 'Came back March 1903. "Undesirable"'.
24. Entry crossed out.
25. Entry crossed out, with remark 'Invalided at the Cape'.
26. This remark, presumably added much later, is probably a reference to Wild's
    membership of Shackleton's *Nimrod* expedition, 1907–9. Markham
    disapproved of that expedition and of those connected with it.
27. Entry crossed out, with remark 'Came back March 1903. "Undesirable"'.
28. Entry crossed out, with same remark as for Page (Note 23).
29. Entry crossed out, with remark 'Came back March 1903'.
30. Entry crossed out, with remark 'Not strong enough. Discharged at Lyttelton'.
31. Entry crossed out, with remark 'Discharged at the Cape'.
32. Entry crossed out, with remark 'Ran at Port Chalmers'.
33. Entry crossed out, with remark 'Discharged at the Cape. Objectionable'.
34. Entry crossed out, with remark 'Came back 1903 (March)'.
35. Entry crossed out, with remark 'Came back March 1903 – Reached England
    11 May'.
36. Entry crossed out, with remark 'Refused to go out'.
37. Entry crossed out, with remark 'Discharged at Lyttelton. Objectionable'.
38. Entry crossed out, with remark 'Came back March 1903. "Undesirable"'.
39. Entry crossed out, with remark 'Discharged at Lyttelton. No good'.
40. Entry crossed out, with remark 'Came back in *Morning* March 1903'.
41. Entry crossed out, with remark 'Discharged at the Cape. Useless'.
42. Markham's footnote; referring to all those marked by *:
    These were on the Joint Committee, with 15 more!
43. Markham's footnote:
    The Ship Committee was appointed by me before the Joint Committee
    existed, and met 11 times – April 10, 17, June 20, Sept 25, Nov 27, Dec 13
    in 1899; 24 Jan; 23 Feb, 1 June, 21 June, 10 Dec 1890, when the work was
    handed over to Scott.
    The Geological Sub-Committee met 4 times – 13 July, 14 Sept, 21 Nov
    1900, and 11 Jan 1901. Result *nil*.
    The Biological Sub-Committee met 3 times – 17 July, 28 Nov 1899, 7 Feb
    1900 – Result *nil*.
    The Hygiene Sub-Committee met twice – 7 May and 10 July 1900. Result
    nil.
    The Meteorological Sub-Committee met once – 19 Nov 1900. Agreed to a

list of instruments, which was altered.

The Magnetic Sub-Committee met twice – 14 July 1899 and 15 Feb 1900, handing all over to Capt Creak.

The Oceanographic Sub-Committee met once – 2 Nov 1900.

The machinery of Sub-Committees proved to be quite useless. I handed over all I wanted them to do to George Murray, as Editor of the Antarctic Manual.

44. Markham's footnote:
   Succeeded by Mr Teall, Geologist.

45. Markham's note:
   Subscribed later.

46. Markham's footnote:
   The thing itself was of no consequence, but I would not allow it to be done without my permission. I had said in a letter that a second doctor would be useful if there was a landing party. He thought this showed inconsistency, having thus referred to a landing party, if I wanted the ship to winter.

47. Markham's footnote:
   The Whartons were of Healaugh in Yorkshire, also in Cumberland and Durham, and produced a line of Barons, ending with the eccentric Duke of Wharton. The Duke's father, Lord Wharton, as a youth, was painted by Vandyke, the most beautiful picture in the Vandyke exhibition of 1900, belonging now to the Emperor of Russia.

   Mr. John Wharton of Aberford, Sir William's uncle, was one of my Father's oldest friends, and was co-executor with my Father, to my uncle Colonel Markham of Becca. His son John Wharton is in Parliament and a Privy Councillor.

   Through his mother's family, the Crofts of Easingwold, thence through to the Hattons of [   ], Sir William Wharton is of royal descent.

SELECTED BIOGRAPHIES

DAVIS, Captain John Edward (1815–77). Davis served as Second Master on HMS *Terror* (Captain F. R. M. Crozier) during James Clark Ross's Antarctic expedition of 1839–43. He later saw Arctic service on the voyage of *Fox* to Iceland and Greenland to investigate the possibility of laying a trans-Atlantic cable. Later in life he lectured widely on polar exploration, and he retired from active naval service only shortly before his death. Some of his work as an artist on Ross's expedition is preserved at the Scott Polar Research Institute.

FOSTER, Sir Michael (1836–1907). From 1867 taught physiology at the University of London, at the Royal Institution and at Cambridge, where he became professor of physiology. Elected FRS 1872 and was its biological secretary from 1881 to 1903. President of the British Association and KCB 1899. MP for University of London 1900–06. Member of the Joint Committee.

GEIKIE, Sir Archibald (1835–1924). Geologist; began making observations in Scotland and in 1855 was appointed a member of the Geological Survey. Became director in Scotland in 1867, and director-general for Britain in 1882. Retired in 1901. Elected a Fellow of the Royal Society in 1865. Served as its foreign secretary 1889–93, secretary 1903–8, and President 1908–12. Knighted 1891, created KCB 1907 and received the OM in 1913. Member of the Expedition's Joint Committee and an opponent of Markham.

GOLDIE, Sir George Dashwood Taubman (1846–1925). Served in the Royal Engineers 1865–7, then travelled extensively in Africa. In 1877 visited the Niger in order to investigate British commercial interests, an occupation which developed into his life's work, and which was later to earn him the reputation of the founder of Nigeria. Created KCMG in 1887. Elected FRS 1902, and elected President of the RGS 1905. Later an alderman of London County Council. A member of the Select Committee of the Expedition and largely responsible for healing the rift between the RS and the RGS.

GREGORY, John Walter (1864–1932). Educated at the University of London and began his scientific career in 1887 as assistant in the Geological Department of the British Museum (Natural History). From 1891 began to travel widely in North America and the West Indies and to publish extensively on geology and palaeontology. In 1892 was naturalist to a large expedition to British East Africa. That expedition was spoiled by various difficulties, but Gregory reorganized it privately to make important studies of Mount Kenya and of the Great Rift Valley. In 1896 he crossed Spitzbergen with Sir Martin Conway. There then followed his acceptance of, and subsequent resignation from, the post of director of the Civilian Staff of the National Antarctic Expedition, the subject of which forms a large part of this book. In December 1900, he was appointed to the Chair of Geology at the University of Melbourne. He later became Director of the Geological Survey in the Mines Department of Victoria. In 1904 he accepted the Chair of Geology in the University of Glasgow, a position which he held until his retirement in 1929. He continued throughout this period to travel widely as a geologist. On 2 June, 1932 he was drowned in the course of an expedition to South America. Elected to the Royal Society 1901. President of the Geological Society 1928–30. He received many other honours for his work.

HAMILTON, Admiral Sir Richard Vesey (1829–1912). Served twice in the Canadian Arctic on expeditions in search of Sir John Franklin's North-west Passage expedition. In 1850–1 he served as mate on HMS *Assistance*, Captain Erasmus Ommanney, and in 1852–4 he served as lieutenant on HMS *Resolute*, Captain Henry Kellett. He was later First Sea Lord (1889–91). He received the GCB and was put on the retired list in 1895. A member of the Joint Committee of the National Antarctic Expedition and a supporter of Markham.

HOSKINS, Sir Anthony Hiley (1828–1901). Entered the Royal Navy 1842 and served off the coasts of Africa and China and on the North American station. Commodore in Australian waters 1875–8. CB 1877; rear-admiral 1879; lord commissioner of the Admiralty from 1880. Commander-in-chief in the Mediterranean 1889–91; admiral and senior naval lord of the Admiralty 1891; retired in 1893 and was nominated GCB in the same year. Member of the Joint Committee and a supporter of Markham.

MARKHAM, Admiral Sir Albert Hastings (1841–1918). Entered the Royal Navy 1856 and served eight years on the China station, then on the Mediterranean and Australian stations. In 1873 sailed on the whaler *Arctic* to Davis Strait. In 1875–6 he was on the British Arctic Expedition, HMS *Alert*, and led a sledge party attempting to reach the North Pole from Ellesmere Island. He attained 83°20′26″N, a record for the time. Visited Novaya Zemlya on a private cruise, 1879, and in 1886 surveyed ice conditions in Hudson Bay and Strait. He was commodore of the training squadron, 1886–90. Rear-admiral 1891; KCB 1903. Retired from the Navy 1906. A member of the Joint Committee and a supporter of Sir Clements Markham, who was his cousin.

NARES, Sir George Strong (1831–1915). Entered the Royal Navy 1845. Later served as midshipman and mate on the Australian station and in the South Pacific. Lieutenant 1852. Served on HMS *Resolute* in the search for Sir John Franklin 1852–54. Promoted Captain RN 1869. Commanded *Challenger* oceanographic expedition to the southern oceans 1872–74, but was then recalled to lead the British Arctic Expedition 1875–76 on HMS *Alert* and *Discovery*, which explored in northern Canada and Greenland. Elected FRS 1875; appointed rear admiral 1887; vice admiral 1892. Member of the Antarctic Expedition's Joint Committee representing the RGS, but later denounced by Markham as a 'deserter' for taking the RS's view over the appointment of Gregory.

OSBORN, Sherard (1822–75). As lieutenant, RN, commanded the steamer *Pioneer* on two voyages to the Canadian Arctic in search of Sir John Franklin's missing North-west Passage expedition; in 1850–1 under the general command of Captain H. T. Austin, and in 1852–4 under Captain Sir Edward Belcher. From January 1865, when he presented a paper before the Royal Geographical Society, until 1874, he repeatedly presented a case for a British expedition to explore towards the North Pole from the region of Smith Sound. The result of his and others' labours was the British Arctic Expedition of 1875–6 (see introduction and NARES). He died on 6 May 1875, shortly before the departure of that expedition.

POULTON, Sir Edward Bagnall (1856–1943). Educated at Oxford where, in 1876 became demonstrator in comparative anatomy. Particular interest was entomology with special reference to markings and protective attitudes of caterpillars. In 1890 produced a seminal book on the colours of animals. Elected Fellow of the RS 1889; appointed Professor of Zoology at Oxford 1893, a position which he held until 1933. Vice-President of the RS 1909–10. Knighted 1935. One of Markham's main opponents over the nature of the National Antarctic Expedition, and a firm and loyal supporter of Gregory. The reasons for his support are presented here in Appendix 2.

RAWSON, Wyatt, Commander, RN (1853–82). As 'one of the foremost and most eager of the volunteers' was appointed 3rd lieutenant of the *Discovery* on the British Arctic Expedition, 1875–6 (see NARES), during which he made several sledging journeys between the *Discovery* at Lady Franklin Bay and the *Alert* on the north coast of Ellesmere Island, and across Robeson Channel to explore the north coast of Greenland with Lieutenant Lewis Beaumont. He died of a bullet wound in the Egyptian campaign of 1882.